"Is it my imagination, or are the police a lot smaller these days?"

UMBRO

SHARP

MANCHESTER UNITED

ning lines...

£5.99

topical times football book 2000

contents

the deadly double–

yorke & cole

tHE very mention of those two names in the same breath is enough to instil fear in the most accomplished defences. Ever since Dwight Yorke and Andy Cole teamed up as Manchester United's striking partnership, they have devastated opposition the length and breadth of the country - and across Europe too.

Cole, the £7 million striker who had made his reputation with a blitz of goals for Newcastle, had blown hot and cold since his arrival at Old Trafford three years earlier. Would a new partner bring the best out of him?

Yorke, after almost a decade at Aston Villa, was fanfared as United's record signing when bought for a massive £12.6 million. How would he handle the huge expectations?

The answers came immediately as the pair hit it off from day one. Week after week, they banged in goals as they both raced to the top of the Premiership scorers' table, yet they took as much delight in creating chances for each other.

Some observers have described their understanding as telepathic. Though Yorke stops short of such a bold assessment, he agrees that his link-up with Cole is 'very special' and made his introduction to life at Old Trafford just perfect.

Says the 27-year-old striker, "It was amazing how quickly we struck up a relationship.

"Until I arrived at United, we hardly knew each other. Of course, we had come across one another at matches during the previous few seasons, but I only knew Andy enough to say 'Hi' to him in passing.

> " People have said it is telepathy. I might not put it as strongly as that, but there is certainly a lot of instinct about our game. "

"It was hardly enough to suggest we would be buddies once I was transferred to Old Trafford.

"Yet from day one we just seemed to hit it off. I think when you first arrive in a new environment, you either get on with people or you don't, and we seemed to take a liking to each other straight away.

"People have said it is telepathy. I might not put it as strongly as that, but there is certainly a lot of instinct about our game.

"When things come off for us, they just happen. We don't sit down beforehand and work out our moves. Neither of us has ever said, 'This is what we are going to do.' Yet we have gone out for matches and somehow known what the other one is going to do or where he will be.

"That is probably what makes this partnership different class.

"I have been very lucky during my career in English football, because I have played alongside some great players. Cyrille Regis, Dean Saunders and David Platt were among my striking partners at Aston Villa. I learned a lot from each of them and considered myself very fortunate to have been able to play with such great players.

"But this partnership is special. When Andy and I go out for a match, we have a huge confidence that we will score goals. We know we are going to get chances at some stage of the game, and I always feel that, if I don't get my name on the scoresheet, Andy will.

"We are always on a high because we score so frequently. And I am just as happy to create a chance for him as I am to be scoring myself. Andy feels just the same - and that is what this partnership is all about." *(Continued over)*

One big difference which splits the pair away from club duty becomes evident in an international week, however. While Cole is busy adding to his tally of England caps and aiming to play in World Cups and European Championships, Yorke is only too aware that he is unlikely to hit such heights while playing for his own country, Trinidad and Tobago.

One of the world's footballing minnows, his place of birth has prevented him from reaching the heights at international level.

But Yorke has no regrets about this and remains as proud of his nationality as any World Cup winner.

He says, "Yes, it's frustrating for me that we are such a small and unsuccessful country in football terms. But I cannot help where I was born and I accept that situation.

"Sometimes I feel as though my whole life has been mapped out for me and I am simply going along with it. But even if that is the case, I certainly can't complain about the route it has taken and the way things have worked out for me, especially when you consider the country I come from and the difficulties I faced while I was growing up.

"Things have changed so enormously for me that, although I'm disappointed that I can't play in World Cups, it's not something that

I will lose sleep over. Being with United gives me the opportunity to play against World Cup players, so turning out for this club is my World Cup and I enjoy it."

Yorke is also proud that he has become a role model for all the kids in his country who love to play football, and hopes that his own success will act as a spur for more of his countrymen to make their mark on the game.

So far, he is Trinidad and Tobago's most famous footballing export, and is keen to use his own fame to further the progress of the game in his homeland.

"I suppose my name has always been bandied about at home since I was a youngster, when I joined Villa," he reflects. "And since I

joined United for such a huge sum of money, it probably made me even more famous.

"But that has not made me a different person. I'm still just a bloke who enjoys playing football and happens to play for the biggest club in the world.

"As far as I know, there had been no previous footballers from my country who made it big. That does put a bit of responsibility on me.

"But I like to think that I have done something to help young footballers in my country who are keen to make something of themselves. It would give me a lot of pleasure to know that my success has encouraged youngsters back home to say, 'If Dwight Yorke has made it, then so can I.' That is the kind of encouragement I hope I can give.

"If there is another young star ready to emerge - and I am positive there must be - I hope he gets the same opportunity as I did, and if I can spur him on through my own success, I'd love that.

"I was still a teenager when Graham Taylor, then manager of Aston Villa, visited the island and saw me play. He must have spotted something in my game and said what everyone had told me - that I had talent.

"He gave me my big opportunity by inviting me over here and I have never looked back since.

"Now I believe that others can take the same route. It is still just as difficult to get a break in football over there, but it is difficult in any walk of life.

"But once you are dedicated and believe in yourself, then you have come through half the battle.

"That is my message to the kids in my homeland who have watched my career and dreamed of doing it themselves." ■

flying the flag

francis **JEFFERS** Everton

TOPICAL TIMES FOOTBALL BOOK

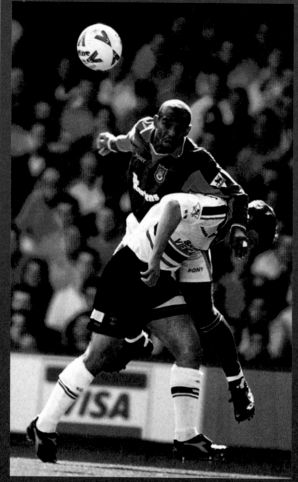

● TREVOR SINCLAIR (West Ham United) and GARY NEVILLE (Manchester United)

double action!

● STEFANO ERANIO (Derby County) and STEPHEN HUGHES (Arsenal)

● ROBBIE FOWLER (Liverpool) and PAUL WILLIAMS (Coventry City)

● TEMURI KETSBAIA (Newcastle United) and DARIO MARCOLIN (Blackburn Rovers)

● STAN LAZARIDIS (West Ham United) and MICHAEL OWEN (Liverpool)

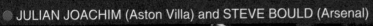
● JULIAN JOACHIM (Aston Villa) and STEVE BOULD (Arsenal)

GIANFRANCO ZOLA wants to get better and better!

GIANFRANCO ZOLA is hoping to prove this year that, like the great wines of his native Italy, he can get better with age. Zola arrived at Chelsea three years ago, and won the Footballer of the Year award in his first season at Stamford Bridge. But last season the Italian felt he was playing even better, at the age of 32. And this year he aims to carry on improving.

''After I was left out of Italy's squad for the World Cup in France, people may have been thinking that, at 32, I had given my best, that I couldn't do any more,'' says Franco.

''But I can give something more. I can still be the best. There is always something to prove in football. Even the best player in the world can always get better. There are no limits.

''The day I feel there is nothing more to prove, is the day I will give up. But that's in the future.

''In the last year Antonio Pintus has done a wonderful job with the training. Since he came to Stamford Bridge as fitness trainer, we have been much fitter.

''It's very tough, but the training sessions are very good. It's not about technique, it's physical work, a lot of running.

''Physically, I'm spot-on. I'm much fitter than I ever was when I played in Italy.

''I feel very good. I can run for ninety minutes. How many matches have we won in the last few minutes with late goals ? Quite a few I think.

''When you are physically very fit, it means you are mentally clear. It gives you a big advantage.

''When you make a run in the 90th minute, the opposition may not be as mentally sharp as you, and therefore more likely to make a mistake.''

Zola has benefitted as much as anyone from the new training regime at Stamford Bridge. After his sensational first season with Chelsea, the Italian's form dropped off slightly, and he lost his international place.

Zola enjoyed a good rest while many of his Chelsea colleagues and even more Premiership opponents were involved in the World Cup finals.

He returned last season sharper than ever, to play his part in Chelsea's title challenge. Zola, like his team-mates at Stamford Bridge, has responded to the prompting of manager Gianluca Vialli. Chelsea have become a more professional team under Vialli.

''If you look at the history of this team, we often have played fantastic against the top teams, and lost against others not so good,'' says Zola.

''In the past, when Chelsea won a big game, we never played as well in the next game. We lost to teams not as strong as us.

''Under Luca, we are more professional, so that problem has gone. He's played for many years in successful teams, and knows the mentality needed.

''When he was a player in Italy, I could see that was the way he was. When you work that way as a player, you will be successful as a manager.

''Luca is a hard man to work for. Football is to be enjoyed, but first you have to work hard.

''You have to be a good athlete to challenge at the highest level. Also you must have the right mentality to treat every game the same way.

''We are working in a certain way at Chelsea. The path we choose is the right one. We believe in that.

''We know we can do big things. Many teams want to be successful, but most of them don't know how to go about it.

''For us it's not a surprise that we are doing well. It's not by chance. Our path is to take care of everything tactically, physically and mentally.

''Luca cares a lot about the players talking together. He thinks if you create a group where everybody communicates, it makes everybody's life much easier.

''In the Premier League, and in European competitions, we come across a lot of different situations. It helps if you can work out these problems as a unit.''

One of the problems Chelsea encountered last season was with the Stamford Bridge pitch. In mid-season it was cutting up badly. Zola went to the club management to ask for action to be taken. The club agreed, and a new playing surface was laid in the space of a week.

''I wasn't the only one to complain about the pitch. We all knew something had to be done,'' reveals Franco. ''It's important to have a good surface to play on.

''It wasn't a question of tiredness on the heavy ground. The work we do in training pays off most when the grounds are at their most tiring, particularly for big strong guys like me!

''But when a pitch is very bumpy it's easier for teams to defend against us. We need a good surface to make the most of our passing ability.''

Zola has been impressed by Vialli's transition

school of excel

from player to manager. But he doesn't foresee the same progression for himself.

''I can't see myself sitting on a bench shouting at someone. I don't think I'll be coach, although you never know,'' he says.

''At the moment I'm very focused on my football. I still really love playing.''

> There is always something to prove in football. Even the best player in the world can always get better.

ience!

Player of the Decade: Alf Common

mULTI-MILLION POUND transfer fees are so frequent these days that we take them for granted. But when Alf Common became the first player to be transferred for £1000 back in 1905, the deal caused an outcry. It even resulted in the Football League placing a limit on transfer fees to prevent such ludicrous business being done again!

Common, a much-travelled centre-forward and an Edwardian-looking character with a bushy moustache, was born in the Millfield district of Sunderland, and began his career with the local club.

He moved to Sheffield United, but later returned to Sunderland for £500 - then a record fee — because he wanted to return to his roots and be close to his business interests.

Very quickly, however, Sunderland sold him to Middlesbrough for double that amount. Sheffield United were peeved that he had been sold on so soon and the whole affair caused great controversy.

A popular sporting newspaper of the day, the Athletic News, shot Middlesbrough down for trying to buy their way out of relegation.

The Teesside club were going through a poor spell and had not won away from home for two years. Yet almost as soon as he pulled on a 'Boro jersey, Common inspired them to a winning performance which ended that unwanted record. He scored the only goal from the penalty spot as Middlesbrough won 1-0 — ironically against Sheffield United at Bramall Lane!

This made United even angrier and they complained to the Football League about Sunderland having sold him so soon just to make a quick profit. The League agreed, and set a ceiling of £850 on future transfer deals.

Common won three caps for England. Once, after travelling to Ireland for an international, where he was an unused reserve, he caught a cold while returning by boat across the Irish Sea. On the following Saturday, his side lost 6-1 to Southampton in the FA Cup and Common blamed his poor performance on the voyage.

After spending his best years with 'Boro, he saw out his career with Preston North End and Woolwich Arsenal, before returning to the North East as a publican.

Other leading players of the 1900s:

STEVE BLOOMER, who scored 292 League goals in two spells with Derby County.

SANDY BROWN, who scored 15 goals in a single Cup run as Tottenham lifted the FA Cup in 1901.

Milestones:

1903. Bury beat Derby County 6-0 to record the highest-ever FA Cup Final score.

1904. FIFA is founded.

1908. Manchester United win the first Charity Shield, beating Queens Park Rangers 4-0, after a 1-1 draw.

---

topical times

a century of soccer

no1. 1900-09 1910-19

Player of the Decade: Billy Meredith

aAT the height of his career - which spanned 28 years - Welshman Billy Meredith was voted the best player in the world. He was also Stanley Matthews' boyhood hero.

Football's first superstar, he made 700 appearances for the Manchester clubs and won 51 caps for Wales, a remarkable achievement in an age when the home countries only played against each other.

One of the game's more colourful characters, his trademark was a Charlie Chaplin moustache and a toothpick which he chewed during matches.

The newly-formed Manchester City first spotted him playing in his hometown of Chirk in North Wales, but angered the locals when it became known that they intended taking their star player away from them.

Tempers became so heated that, in one frightening exchange, one member of the City deputation was dragged through a horse trough by protesters.

But City secured their man, and he captained them to victory in the FA Cup in 1904, when he scored the only goal of final against Bolton Wanderers.

Meredith later joined local rivals United, where he enjoyed greater success in the form of two League Championships and another FA Cup win.

After 15 years with United, however, he returned to City for the last three years of his career.

As chairman at the inaugural meeting of the Players' Union in Manchester in 1907, he was also to become a leading figure in the way football was to be run.

He was also responsible for amending the penalty rule, which had previously allowed goalkeepers to advance to the six-yard line. In one game, Meredith calmly flicked the ball over the keeper's head, and the rule was changed.

Milestones:

1912. The UK win the Olympic gold for football in Stockholm.

1919. The Football League is extended to 44 clubs.

15

des

An FA Cup Final is

MAYBE NEXT TIME!

perate den!

a must for Arsenal's DENNIS BERGKAMP

ARSENAL striker Dennis Bergkamp may bow out of international football next summer. The Dutchman plans to depart with a flourish, by helping Holland to win the Euro 2000 Championships, which are being held jointly in Belgium and in his homeland.

However, Bergkamp hopes to extend his contract at Arsenal, so that he can end his playing career at Highbury and achieve one final ambition. The target is that elusive FA Cup winner's medal. He missed out through injury in '98, when the Gunners beat Newcastle United in the final.

Then last season, the Dutch star was heartbroken to lose the semi-final replay in extra time to Manchester United after seeing his penalty saved by Peter Schmeichel in the last seconds of normal time.

Bergkamp is desperate to be involved in the FA Cup final at Wembley. He was in the Arsenal party last year, and was even presented later with a special medal. But he didn't really feel part of the occasion.

But first he has the European Championship Finals in his sights.

"I'd really like to achieve something on home soil," says Dennis. "We've had a good side for a few years now, and it would be good to show it by winning the European Championship.

"That will probably be my last international tournament, and I want to make it special. Of course, you never know what will happen with the national team, but we are good enough to win it.

"I have another year at Arsenal, after this one. I don't know what will happen then, but I won't make a decision for another year.

"It is certainly an option to finish my career at Highbury. At the moment that's what I feel I'd like to do. Arsenal want to build a team, and achieve something over a few years, so the team can be successful for a period of time. In Italy, you have to be successful in one season. Then they think about the next season. It's not the same.

"I think it's good to have a system that works, and can be developed. You can't just rely on one or two players.

"It is all much more relaxed in England. It's easier to get motivated.

"There is time to spend with the family, whereas in Italy it is football, football, football all the time. Seven days a week, very intense.

"The game is played differently here. The fans expect teams to play attacking football all the time.

"You go out to win matches. The attitude is always the same, whether you are at the top or the bottom of the table.

"In Italy, a draw is often enough. They don't try for anything more. I found it strange when I went there from Ajax. I wasn't used to that kind of approach.

"Also, in Italy the people want to talk about the game yesterday, the game next week, and everything in between. There's no break from football.

"I'm very relaxed in England, playing my sort of football, and being successful. That's my idea of life."

Even as a youngster in Holland, Bergkamp was fascinated by the glamour of the FA Cup. He wants to experience the Wembley atmosphere as a player.

"Cup Final day was always very special for me when I was a kid growing up in Holland. There was four or five hours coverage on Dutch television," he recalls.

"You looked forward to the whole day. It's the biggest club match in the world. That's why the final is so special to me.

"When I look back on my career in a few years time, it would be nice to be able to remember playing in the FA Cup final. Missing the game last year was the greatest disappointment of my career.

"I was given a medal, but it wasn't the same as playing in the match. It's true that I didn't really feel part of it on the day.

"I can understand why people say the championship is more important. But the FA Cup has meant a lot to me for a long time."

Bergkamp has been a great example to the young players at Arsenal in his dedicated approach to training and the practice of skills. He is happy to pass on his knowledge.

"I was privileged to play alongside Marco Van Basten for Ajax and Holland. I learned a lot from playing and training with him," says Dennis.

"He was one of the players I admired and looked up to, even when I was playing with him. It's important for young players to have someone as a role model.

"Young defenders at Manchester United can learn from Jaap Stam. He's a great player, very fast and strong. I knew that Jaap would be very successful in English football. At club level he's a very difficult opponent, but it's great to play in front of him for Holland.

"I hope we can help our national team to win the European Championship next summer." ■

> **"When I look back on my career in a few years time, it would be nice to be able to remember playing in the FA Cup final. Missing the game last year was the greatest disappointment of my career."**

giovanni **VAN BRONCKHORST** Rangers

TOPICAL TIMES FOOTBALL BOOK

F you were to ask Alex Ferguson the most vital moment in Manchester United's glorious Treble-winning season, he might point to Peter Schmeichel's penalty save in the FA Cup semi-final against Arsenal. Or, he might choose the enforced substitution of Teddy Sheringham for Roy Keane in the Final of that competition. And there was also United's comeback in the Champions League clash with Juventus in Turin, when goals from Keane, Yorke and Cole clawed back a two-goal deficit. Manchester United fans will have their own golden moment from last season too. We've put together our own selection of highlights...one not directly involving United...which we feel contributed in some way to the historic Treble.

"glory, glory man.

December 26th, 1998. United 3. Nottingham Forest 0. This was United's first win in seven games and their first clean sheet in twelve. Two goals by Ronnie Johnsen and one by Ryan Giggs eased the Reds through and more than made up for a 3-2 home defeat by Middlesbrough the week before. This was the start of a 33-match unbeaten run.

united"

January 24th, 1999. FA Cup 4th Round. United 2, Liverpool 1. An early goal from Michael Owen had sent the Anfield side well on the way to a hard-fought win over their great rivals. Time was running out for Fergie's men until Dwight Yorke grabbed an equaliser in the dying minutes. Then up popped substitute Ole Gunnar Solskjaer to fire home the winner in time added on. United's cup dream was still alive!

April 14th, 1999. FA Cup semi-final replay, Villa Park. United 2, Arsenal 1 (after extra time). This match will be long-remembered for Ryan Giggs' marvellous match-winner, when a mazy run left Arsenal defenders trailing in his wake before he lashed the ball high past David Seaman. However, United might have been down and out in normal time had not Peter Schmeichel pulled off a last-minute penalty save from Dennis Bergkamp. Now, only one team could do the Double!

May 11th, 1999. Leeds United 1, Arsenal 0. Arsenal knew a defeat here would effectively end their hopes of retaining the Championship. United had a game in hand over the Highbury side and were already a point ahead. A late goal from Jimmy Floyd Hasselbaink earned three points for the home side and gave United a boost in the title run-in.

May 16th, 1999. United 2, Spurs 1. The last game of the season. United led Arsenal by two points and knew a win would see them Champions. However, nerves were there for all to see and it was Spurs who silenced the 55,000 crowd by taking the lead through Les Ferdinand. A David Beckham rocket levelled things and in 47 minutes Andy Cole sent the fans into raptures when he lobbed Ian Walker for the Championship clincher.

CARLING CHAMPION '99

CARLING CHAMPIONS 1998-99

May 22nd, 1999. FA Cup Final. United 2, Newcastle 0. Ferguson opted for a strike force of Cole and Solskjaer for this match, but an injury to captain Roy Keane saw Teddy Sheringham come on in his place. Perhaps not an inspired substitution, but a vital one. It took only 90 seconds for Sheringham to fire the Reds ahead from a Paul Scholes through ball. Scholes added a second in the second half to kill off any Newcastle hopes of a fightback. The Double was done!

United were flying and it was perhaps fitting that it was on Concorde that the United squad flew to Barcelona and their date with destiny... the Champions League Final against Bayern Munich. Could they complete an unprecedented Treble?

May 26th, 1999. Champions League Final. United 2, Bayern Munich 1. Few will argue that this match had one of the most dramatic conclusions ever seen. Trailing to a sixth-minute goal from Mario Basler, United could not find the equaliser. Indeed, they were lucky not to go further behind when shots from Mehmet Scholl and Carsten Jancker came off the woodwork. Then came Fergie's inspired masterstrokes. Sheringham and Solskjaer replaced Blomqvist and Cole. They were into time added on when Sheringham turned in the box to sweep the ball past Oliver Kahn. Hardly had the celebrations died down when Sheringham flicked on a Beckham corner for Solskjaer to stab the ball home. Now the celebrations could start! United had become the first side to do the Premiership, FA Cup and Champions League Treble.

The England player with

that contine touch

fOR several years, various England managers have toyed with the idea of using a Continental-style sweeper system. The main problem has been finding the right man to fill the demanding role of sweeper. Such players have been few and far between. Now, it looks like the right man has arrived on the scene...West Ham United's Rio Ferdinand. He is a ball-playing defender capable of keeping things secure at the back, but skilful and confident enough to bring the ball out of defence, creating an extra man in midfield. Ferdinand likes the idea of playing as a sweeper for England. But he is content just to be in the international set-up.

"Ideally I'd like to play as a sweeper, but it's up to the manager to decide on the system. I'm not in a position to stipulate about where I want to play," says Rio.

"I'm happy to play anywhere, but I do enjoy the challenge of trying to build from the back. At West Ham I am encouraged to play that way... pass and move, pass and move.

"The manager always wants you to pass the ball, but there are times when you just have to boot it clear.

"It's the same with bringing the ball out. You have to pick and choose your moment. The situation determines when you can do it.

"I notice the buzz from the fans when I go forward. It's great to hear the reaction. But I never think 'I'll do this for the fans'."

Ferdinand accepts that his style of play has a high-risk factor. It can lead to the occasional costly mistake. Rio accepts the 'stick' that comes from giving away goals but his aim is to make as few mistakes as possible.

"Criticism is part and parcel of football. I try to look at it in a positive way," he says.

"I know you can't expect to play well in every single game, or go through a season without making any errors. I just try to be as near perfect as possible.

"I want to be the best. I'm no different to anyone else. It plays on my mind if I have a bad game, and I try to put it right in the next match."

The young Londoner had his first setback at the time of his initial selection for the senior England squad. A drink-driving incident led to Glenn Hoddle leaving him out of the international set-up.

It was a painful, but valuable experience.

"I didn't like it at the time, but it was a positive thing for me," admits Rio. "The whole business opened my eyes to how much you are in the public eye as a footballer. It makes you realise where you are in life, and what your responsibilities are."

Where Rio Ferdinand is right

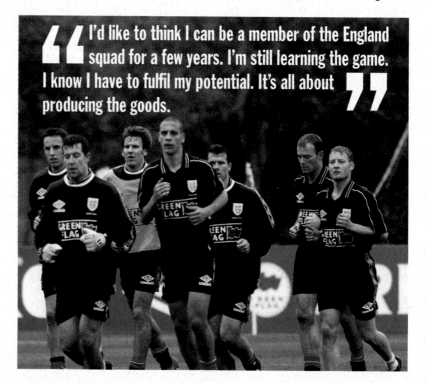

> " I'd like to think I can be a member of the England squad for a few years. I'm still learning the game. I know I have to fulfil my potential. It's all about producing the goods. "

ntal

now, he has the football world at his feet. His responsibility is to show the world that English defenders can be skilled in control and use of the ball, as well as tough in the tackle, and strong in the air.

Although he didn't play in the Finals, the young Londoner learned much from the sidelines during the World Cup in France.

In fact, on his return, Ferdinand was just as tired as any of the players who took part in England's four matches.

"I was mentally drained at the end of the World Cup," he says. "I was exhausted by the whole experience.

"Even though I didn't play, I was concentrating the whole time. I was focusing on things, trying to learn, trying to make sure I would be ready if I was called on.

"It was frustrating to be on the bench. I wanted to be out there, playing in the World Cup.

"But it was still a great experience, something I'll treasure for the rest of my career. And of course, next time I hope to be playing. I feel time is on my side. The European Championships are ahead, and I hope we can still qualify for the finals.

"I'd like to think I can be a member of the England squad for a few years. I'm still learning the game. I know I have to fulfil my potential. It's all about producing the goods.

"I set myself goals at the start of each season. I've done that every year since my YTS days at West Ham.

"I try to fulfil my goal each year, and so far things have gone pretty well. Each year I've aimed a bit higher, and managed to achieve the target. If you don't have goals in your career you can lose ambition. I don't intend letting that happen to me." ∎

aston Villa's Lee Hendrie never had any doubts that he wanted to play football for England. As the son of a Scot, the young midfielder could have taken his international chances north of the border. But the Birmingham-born youngster always knew that he would choose England, if and when the time came. That chance came very quickly. He was just 17 when he went on as a sub for the England Under-21s against Croatia, in April, 1996. Lee's career went through some ups and downs over the next two years. Then, one day last season, manager John Gregory called him into his office to hear some big news.

"The gaffer told me that Glenn Hoddle had called me up for the full England squad," says Lee. "I was shocked to bits.

"There had been plenty of speculation about me being selected, but I'd tried not to pay too much attention to that. I just thought I'd be in the Under-21 squad as usual.

"My dad, Paul, had said there was a good chance I'd get the call. Although he's Scottish, he was still delighted for me.

"He didn't mind that I'd chosen to play for England. Dad just wanted what was best for me.

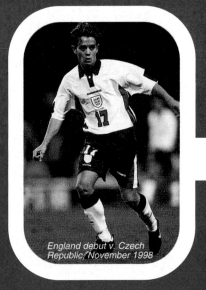

England debut v. Czech Republic, November 1998

LEE HENDRIE'S switch from City to Villa.

"When I was younger, there had been talk of the Scots taking a look at me. But that was something to fall back on, because I always knew I wanted to play for England.

"I don't think I'd ever get my dad to support England against Scotland, but he was with me all the way on that decision. Nobody has had a bigger influence on my career and he's like a brother in many ways.

"He was a good player himself for Birmingham and is a manager at non-League level. Football's in the family because my uncle, John Hendrie, played for Middlesbrough and Barnsley."

Lee's career has been full of divided loyalties. He comes from a family of Birmingham City fans but when he was fifteen he caused uproar by joining Villa.

"I took a lot of stick for that, but it was all quite friendly," says Lee.

"Before that I'd been a Birmingham fan and been on their books as a schoolboy.

"When I joined Villa, I had to switch my colours. The whole family were Blues fans but in the end even my gran bought a Villa season ticket so she could watch me play every week.

"It took me a while to get established at Villa after I'd first broken into the team when I was seventeen. For a while Brian Little, the manager at the time, didn't want to throw me in at the deep end.

"Villa were going through a bad patch near the bottom of the Premiership at the time. He thought there would be too much pressure on me in that situation.

"I was desperate to play but thought I might have to drop down a division. Those are the sort of thoughts you have when you're left out of the team."

Then things changed dramatically at Villa Park when Brian Little resigned and John Gregory arrived in his place. That was good news for Hendrie.

"My career changed direction at that point. I'd been feeling pretty low about my prospects but after John arrived I had a great run in the team.

"If he hadn't arrived when he did I might well have left the club. Thankfully, that didn't happen.

"The gaffer is like one of the lads. But he's definitely got his rules and if he sees somebody stepping out of line he'll come down on them very hard.

"Reputations don't count for much with John. He's not afraid to make changes if a player's not doing his job...whoever he is.

"I think John likes me in the team because I'm always prepared to work hard and never stop trying to create things. When we're under the cosh, I always do what I can to get the team out of trouble.

"The gaffer always says that if you work hard, you get the rewards in the end. My big reward last season was that surprise call to play for England.

"My great England heroes were David Platt and Paul Gascoigne. I used to love watching those two playing in internationals.

"I was a bit nervous when I first joined up with the squad. But I soon started to enjoy myself and when I actually went on to the pitch it was unbelievable.

"That just showed how quickly things can change. I wouldn't have believed it a year earlier but anything can happen in football." ■

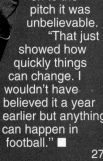

bUYING a foreign player can be a notoriously tricky business. Every manager knows that for every agent offering him a Dennis Bergkamp or a Gianfranco Zola, there are ten others just waiting to take him and his club for a ride. It is a huge gamble.

Even if the hours spent travelling to far-flung places in search of new talent do throw up someone keen to prove themselves in the English game, there is no guarantee of success. Some of the greatest talents in the world have failed to settle in this country.

They may have superb technique, but can they overcome the physical nature of the football, the strange language and the decidedly unfriendly climate? There are so many pitfalls.

However, signing a Dutchman can prove to be less of a risk. Possessing calm temperaments, linguistic skills and a decent knowledge of our game, the likes of Bergkamp and Marc Overmars at Arsenal and Jaap Stam at Manchester United have enjoyed success in England.

That is why Manchester City felt they had nothing to worry about when they signed Gerard Wiekens from Veendam back in 1997. Well-built, unflappable and with a decent touch, he appeared to be just the job for a club desperate to return to the Premiership.

However, by the end of the following season, City had fallen through the trapdoor to the Second Division for the first time in their history. Wiekens had, by his own admission, struggled to establish himself.

Yet he reckons he wasn't to blame. Instead, he points the finger at the British quarantine laws!

Says Gerard, "Some people may laugh, but my first six months at City were really hard because my golden retriever dog, Joey, was in quarantine. For that whole period it was impossible to lead a normal life.

"The centre where the dog was held is in Crewe, which is an hour's drive from Manchester.

"After I'd trained in the morning, showered and had something to eat, it was mid-afternoon before I could get to Crewe. I'd spend an hour with Joey so that meant I wasn't getting home until early evening.

"I did this four times a week for six months. It was difficult to find time to get to know Manchester or my new team-mates.

"This was on top of all the usual problems you'd associate with moving to a new club in a different country. There was so little time even to find somewhere to live. It was really tough.

"It was a distressing period because I'm very attached to my dog, as he is to me, and it wasn't nice for either of us when I had to leave the dog-holding centre to go home. I don't know if it affected my football but I do know I'd have felt a whole lot better if I'd had Joey with me.

"Certainly I'd have had more time to get to know people if I hadn't been going to and from to the centre all the time. Perhaps I would have got used to things quicker and played to my potential earlier than I did."

As if his canine problems weren't bad enough, he also had to come to terms with a club in deep trouble.

He goes on, "City had almost 60 professionals on the books when I arrived and the majority of them had played games in the first team. Every week I'd bump into someone who I thought had just arrived at the club when, in fact, they'd been here all the time.

"As the new boy, it made things hard. Trying to remember all their names was impossible. I often wanted to shout instructions during games but couldn't recall names in time.

"On top of that, I was played out of position. I'd been a defender in Holland but when I came to City, I found myself in midfield.

"It was only after Joe Royle took over from Frank Clark as manager that I returned to my true position. I'm far happier at the back and I've played my best football since being there.

"Being relegated in my first season wasn't ideal. I moved to City believing I had a good chance of getting into the Premier League. Instead I found myself in the Second Division.

"I didn't have any regrets over my move to England, however. Relegation was bitterly disappointing, but thankfully we bounced straight back to Division One via the play-offs last May.

"Next stop, the Premiership!" ■

going to the dogs!

... but things are looking up for Manchester City's GERARD WIEKENS

david **GINOLA** Tottenham Hotspur

TOPICAL TIMES FOOTBALL BOOK

the best of british

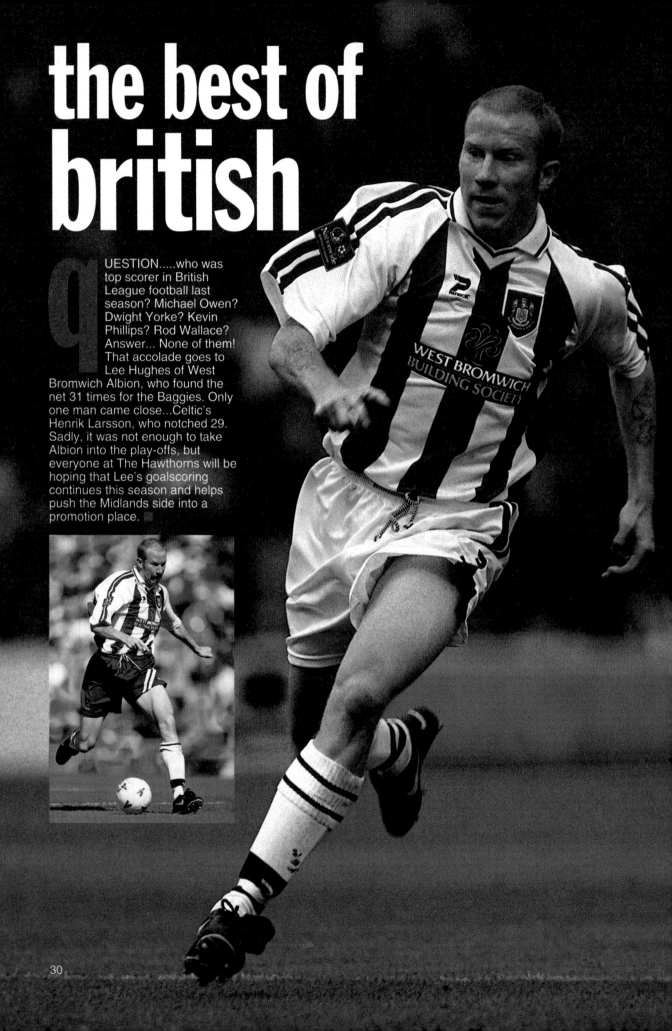

QUESTION.....who was top scorer in British League football last season? Michael Owen? Dwight Yorke? Kevin Phillips? Rod Wallace? Answer... None of them! That accolade goes to Lee Hughes of West Bromwich Albion, who found the net 31 times for the Baggies. Only one man came close...Celtic's Henrik Larsson, who notched 29. Sadly, it was not enough to take Albion into the play-offs, but everyone at The Hawthorns will be hoping that Lee's goalscoring continues this season and helps push the Midlands side into a promotion place.

See 10 across

crossword

across

6 Graham Taylor's 1999 Premiership new boys (7)
7 Arsenal's nickname (7)
9 Barry, boss of Barnet, Southend, Birmingham and Peterborough (3)
10 Midfielder Di Matteo (7)
11 Republic winger Damien (4)
12 USA keeper Friedel (4)
15 What an ace goal poacher does (6)
17 Soccer boss Wenger (6)
18 Johan Cruyff's son (5)
20 Welsh striker Hartson (4)
23 Manchester United's triple-triumph keeper (5,10)
25 Ipswich (4)
26 Stopped by the keeper (5)
28 Blackburn's Matt finisher (6)
30 Jason, team-mate of the above (6)
31 Take this when your side goes ahead (4)
33 Leeds' young striker Smith (4)
35 Welsh side from the Vetch Field (7)
36 England midfielder Parlour (3)
38 What every team wants to be! (7)
39 Republic's wing back Jason (7)

down

1 Club side, Croatia (6)
2 Derby defender Spencer (5)
3 Country where Sturm Graz play (7)
4 The Stretford... (3)
5 ...and the Old ground where you find it (8)
8 In short, an Albion and their home ground (4,4,9)
11 English county that's home of the League's only Argyle (5)
13 What every chairman wants! (7)
14 Country of the Laudrup brothers (7)
16 Kick to the keeper from a defender (8)
19 Vialli, Carbone and Zola (8)
21 Liverpool's Owen (7)
22 The last English team to win the European Cup Winners' Cup (7)
24 England defender Martin (5)
27 Charlton (8)
29 England keeper Tim (7)
32 Villa midfielder Mark (6)
34 Place for a sub to sit (5)
37 The number traditionally worn by a first choice keeper (3)

answers

31

a century of soccer
no.2 1920-29 1930-39

(**Player of the decade: Dixie Dean**)

Photo: Hulton Getty

EW strikers in the modern game would fancy the prospect of facing Arsenal in the final League match of the season needing to score a hat-trick in order to break an all-time goalscoring record.But that was the challenge which faced Everton legend Dixie Dean when he lined up against the Gunners on May 5, 1928.The Birkenhead-born striker had already notched 57 goals for Everton that season and was in sight of the record held by George Camsell, who had scored 59 for Middlesbrough in the Second Division the previous year.

Everton were already within a whisker of clinching the Championship. Arsenal, despite falling away in the last few weeks, had been serious challengers for most of the campaign and still had one of the best defences in the League.

No defence held any fear, however, for a man whose international career yielded 18 goals in just 16 matches for England.

With five minutes remaining, Dean had scored twice to equal the record, and the teams were level at 2-2. Then Everton won a corner. Dean leaped above the Arsenal defence and his header found the back of the net to clinch the Championship and a scoring record of 60 goals in a season, which still stands today.

Thousands of Everton fans were ready to invade the pitch, so Dean asked the referee to tip him off when the final whistle was about to blow, and he smartly nipped off ten seconds before the end to avoid being mobbed!

Born William Ralph Dean, the striker joined Tranmere Rovers in 1924 at 16 years of age and scored 27 goals in 27 games in his first season. But his glory years were spent at Everton where he notched 349 goals in 399 games. He also scored 37 hat-tricks in his career.

In 1928, he was offered the chance to play for the New York Giants for £25 per week, but despite never earning more than £8 per week in his career, he refused to leave Goodison Park.

Eventually, he joined Notts County to round off his career, bringing his overall goal tally to 355.

In 1976, he died while watching an Everton match at his beloved Goodison. ▪

Milestones:

1920. The Third Division (South) is formed, followed by the Third Division (North) a year later.
1923. Wembley stages its first FA Cup Final, the famous "White Horse" Final. Bolton Wanderers beat West Ham United 2-0. An estimated 200,000 fans tried to get in.
1926. Huddersfield Town win the League Championship for the third season running.
1927. Cardiff City beat Arsenal 1-0 in the FA Cup Final to take the trophy out of England for the only time in the competition's history.

Other prominent players of the 1920s:

JIMMY McGRORY. Scored 397 goals for Celtic including 49 in season 1926-27.
DAVID JACK. Scored for Bolton in the FA Cup Final victory of 1923, before going on to star in Arsenal's all-conquering side of the late 1920s and 30s. First £10,000 transfer, Bolton to Arsenal in 1928.

O N FA Cup Final Day in 1930, thousands of pairs of eyes turned skywards as the Graf Zeppelin airship appeared overhead. It was one of the most famous images generated by this most famous of football occasions.

Yet just as many eyes that day were transfixed by a figure down below on the Wembley pitch.

Alex James was in devastating form. The impish Scottish forward terrorised Huddersfield Town's defence and scored once himself as he inspired Arsenal to a 2-0 victory.

One of the game's most flamboyant personalities, James cut a distinctive figure. Just 5ft 6in tall, he went through his entire professional career wearing the baggiest shorts in

football, which flapped about below his knees.

Alex James was also the most influential member of the Arsenal side which swept all before them in the 1930s and came to be known as Napoleon in Baggy Shorts.

Snapped up from Preston North

End for a bargain £8,750 in 1929, he was already assured of legendary status in his native Scotland, having played in the side which beat England 5-1 at Wembley a year earlier, earning them the nickname "The Wembley Wizards."

A prolific goalscorer with Preston, the Highbury club transformed Alex into a goalmaker, and his fellow Arsenal forwards - Joe Hulme, Cliff Bastin, David Jack and Jack Lambert - profited week after week from his brilliant passing.

But manager Herbert Chapman had to keep a firm rein on the wee magician who was fond of turning the football pitch into his personal stage and indulging in his series of party tricks with the ball. Chapman introduced a strict rule whereby James had to cut out the circus act until Arsenal were leading 3-0!

James helped Arsenal win the Championship four times and the FA Cup twice. ■

Photos: Hulton Getty

Player of the decade: Alex James

Other prominent players of the 1930s:

FRANK SWIFT. The first goalkeeper to captain England, the Manchester City star won 19 caps. His finest hour came in a famous 4-0 victory over Italy in Turin. Helped City win the 1935 FA Cup Final, but was so overcome he fainted before going up the Wembley steps to receive his medal from King George V.

TED DRAKE. Arsenal forward who scored 134 League goals for the club, including 42 in one season. Scored all seven in one game against Aston Villa in 1935.

CLIFF BASTIN. His 33 goals in 42 League games for Arsenal during season 1932-33 was a new record for a winger. His career record of 176 goals for the club was only recently broken by Ian Wright.

Milestones:

1930. Uruguay are the first winners of the World Cup.

1933. Players wear numbers for the first time, in the FA Cup Final between Everton and Manchester City, but are numbered from 1 to 22.

1935. Arsenal complete a hat-trick of successive League Championships. They win the title five times in the decade.

1938. East Fife are the first Second Division club to win the Scottish Cup.

1938. New pitch markings, as an arc is added to the edge of the penalty area.

Cliff Bastin

Ted Drake

33

stretch for it!

● DON HUTCHISON, EVERTON and DARREN WILLIAMS, SUNDERLAND

● DAVID BURROWS, COVENTRY

● JASON EUELL, WIMBLEDON

● STEVE STAUNTON, LIVERPOOL and CHRIS ARMSTRONG, SPURS

"we're on our way to wembley!"

When Paul Dobbie and his son David, of Blaydon-on-Tyne, took in the Dunston Federation Brewery against Durham City FA Cup pre-qualifying tie last September, little did they know that this was the start of a 5,200-mile trek that would finish on May 23rd at Wembley at the FA Cup Final!

When Dunston lost 2-0, they became Durham fans and when City lost 4-1 in the next round, the Dobbies decided to switch allegiance to the winners. In fact, they vowed to follow that plan all season, meaning they would see a match in every round of the Cup including the Final itself.

The TOPICAL TIMES spoke to Paul about their epic journey...

TTFB: What was your wife's initial reaction to your planned Wembley trek? Did she think you were daft?! Was she supportive? Or did the enthusiasm wane after a few matches?

PD: I think the best way to describe Beverley's reaction was that she was quietly supportive. She's not really into football these days - although we did meet at Roker Park - but she is happy for David and I to indulge. I asked her the other week if she thought we would see it through and she said she never doubted us!

Continued overleaf

David soaks up the atmosphere before the Evenwood v Durham match in the first qualifying round. The score – Evenwood Town 4 Durham City 1.

TTFB: Worst moment?
PD: Not really had one. Perhaps arriving at Radcliffe Borough on a foul day to hear the ref was still to inspect the pitch but the game went ahead so we didn't have a wasted journey. Also a bad moment which was also quite funny was at Burscough for the Evenwood match. Two kids lost interest and were poking a stick in a hole in a wall behind us. It turned out to be a wasps' nest and of course out they swarmed. The kids were stung and a number of us had to run for cover. I think most of the crowd was watching the panic and the match was just going on in the background.

TTFB: How much did this all cost?
PD: We have not kept accounts but reckon the whole thing was probably pushing £2,000 but it has been money well spent. We thoroughly enjoyed the whole experience, saw some great games and met some smashing people with whom we plan to stay in touch. Football really is a common language.

TTFB: Would you do it again?!
PD: Who knows, but really you can never go back in life. I find when you try you get disappointed. Perhaps it's best to have done it once and hang on to the great memories of a once-in-a-lifetime experience.

David with some of the Telford United team, including (left) Scott Huckerby whose brother Darren we were to see in later rounds.

TTFB: 50 goals...which was the best and/or the most important?
PD: We saw some cracking goals. In the second round proper Tomlinson scored a hat-trick for Macclesfield including a couple of solo runs. In round three Huckerby was on fire for Coventry and scored a hat-trick, again a couple of mazy runs. Then Noel Whelan curled a cracker from the corner of the Leicester penalty area in round four. Gary McAllister bent a free kick into the top corner at Everton in round five and David Unsworth smashed a cracker against Newcastle. But up there among the best, and probably the most important, was Alan Shearer's second strike against Tottenham in the semi-final, (above). That really sealed the game and sent the Toon Army barmy!

TTFB: How many miles did you and your son total and what was the longest journey?
PD: We travelled 5,200 miles which is less than we imagined. It is a long way from Tyneside to most grounds so we were lucky with the draw. It is exciting watching FA Cup draws anyway but when you face the prospect of an 800 mile round trip to Torquay the adrenaline really flows. The furthest we travelled for a single game was Wembley at 600 miles. After that it was to Telford (twice) for a 450-mile round trip.

TTFB: Best moment?
PD: Loads. Every time we had a good draw in terms of travel. At Telford in the first round proper we were guests of the club and wrote a piece in the programme. This was because we used to live there and David was a regular at The Bucks Head. At Macclesfield we were made exceptionally welcome and were invited into the changing rooms after the match to meet some of the players and officials. David had pictures taken with the goalscorers. We were even invited to stay for dinner but were unfortunately unable to stay. Getting an invite to the Leicester-Coventry game from Neil Pickles who has an executive box. With it being a local derby and a small ground we were struggling for tickets. We were on Radio Five Live and Neil stepped in with his kind offer to keep the run going. Getting tickets from Newcastle for the sixth round and semi-final was also a big bonus.

TTFB: Best ground?
PD: Probably Old Trafford, but St James' Park is also pretty impressive. In the early rounds we were impressed by Burscough's home and Durham City's New Ferens Park is just a few years old.

TTFB: Funniest moment?

PD: Apart from the wasps there were a couple of others. One was at Telford for the Burscough game where, in spite of a 500 gate in a 4,000 capacity ground, someone managed to spill their beef tea down my back! At Burscough against Evenwood a ball down the line set up a 50-50 challenge right in front of us. David yelled to the defender to "Whack it away, you stupid knacker" and he did – straight into David's face! Also in that game the referee awarded a penalty to Burscough when the winger had danced round the fullback but stepped on the ball. I think he was the only guy who didn't see what happened.

TTFB: Of all the teams you supported, were there any whose performances made you think "I'd like to support them full-time"?

PD: Probably Burscough again from the non-League sides. They have some very promising young players. Macclesfield too were hard to resist because of the friendly atmosphere at the club. As a Sunderland supporter I could never say I would follow Newcastle but to experience the passion and belief of the supporters close up was great. It's already been said but they deserve better.

TTFB: Which club supplied the best grub?!

PD: It would have to be the full Sunday lunch served up by Newcastle when we were the club's guests for the Everton game. However in terms of pies etc. there was not really anywhere that stood out. The best chips we had were from a chippy outside Goodison Park. We had them before and after the match!

TTFB: As you sift through all the programmes you collected, which memory remains strongest?

PD: There are so many it is difficult to say. The warmth of the welcome at Macclesfield. The day out at Leicester and being interviewed by Alan Birchenal before the game and David being presented with a signed football. Standing on the pitch at Goodison before the match. The sheer noise and emotion at the end of the semi-final. Seeing the twin towers at Wembley and soaking up the pre-match atmosphere.

TTFB: Has there been any media reaction, national or local, to your travels?

PD: Yes, we have had a fair bit of local newspaper, radio and television coverage which was also good fun. We also did Radio Five Live twice - including on the morning of the final with Jack Cunningham - and made it into the Sunday Post, the Weekly News, the Daily Star and the Sport, would you believe!

TTTFB: Did you meet anyone else who had undertaken a similar route to Wembley?

PD: We met George Betteridge from Canterbury, who followed the trail from the qualifying round one. Unfortunately he was unaware of the pre-qualifying or preliminary round. It was great to meet him and we plan to meet again for a longer chat when he travels to Newcastle on business.

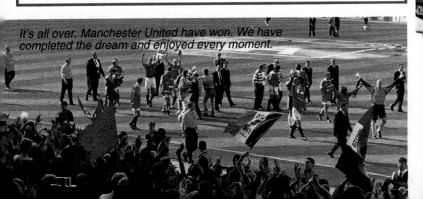

It's all over. Manchester United have won. We have completed the dream and enjoyed every moment.

the Dobbies' route to wembley...

September 4th. Pre-qualifying.
Durham City 2 Dunston Federation Brewery 0

September 19th. First qualifying round.
Evenwood Town 4 Durham City 1

October 3rd. Second qualifying round.
Burscough 2 Evenwood Town 2

October 7th.
Replay. Evenwood Town 0 Burscough 6

October 17th. Third qualifying round.
Radcliffe Borough 0 Burscough 1

November 1st. Fourth qualifying round.
Telford United 2 Burscough 1

November 15th. First round proper.
Telford United 0 Cambridge United 2

December 5th. Second round.
Macclesfield Town 4 Cambridge United 1

January 2nd. Third round.
Coventry City 7 Macclesfield Town 0

January 23rd. Fourth round.
Leicester City 0 Coventry City 3

February 13th. Fifth round.
Everton 2 Coventry City 1

March 7th. Sixth round.
Newcastle United 4 Everton 1

April 11th. Semi-final.
Newcastle United 2 Tottenham Hotspur 0 (Old Trafford)

May 22nd. Final.
Manchester United 2 Newcastle United 0 (Wembley)

hot-spur!

The man who puts his heart and SOL

SOL CAMPBELL is the one defender that every Premiership manager would like in his team. There are a few in Italy and Spain who wouldn't mind the big man in their eleven either. Every year, without fail, Campbell is the subject of multi-million pound transfer speculation from home and abroad.

Since Jaap Stam's £10 million move to Manchester United, the very best defenders have become high-priced commodities and the England man would command a huge fee if Spurs ever decided to let him go.

Tottenham fans have known for a long time that their captain is one of the best in the business. His commanding displays in the heart of their defence have often got the team out of trouble.

But he realises that there is still a lot of hard work to be done before he can take anything for granted.

"There's no point in rushing yourself in this game, "says Sol." I've still got time to become a better footballer at club and international level.

"In between the big international games, Premiership football has to be the main priority for me. That's something you have to be up for week after week, even on a cold, wet night in the middle of winter."

That point was forced home to Sol and his Spurs team-mates last season when George Graham arrived at White Hart Lane to take over as manager. A renowned disciplinarian, Graham stood for no nonsense as he started to lick his new charges into shape.

Sol wasn't complaining. He didn't mind the hard work because the benefits soon became obvious.

"George is a man who likes to win and hates losing," says Sol. "Thankfully, after he arrived we were doing more of one and less of the other than in previous seasons.

"Personally I thought I was playing well before George arrived. The big difference was that he brought better results with him.

"There's no point in playing well yourself if the team keeps losing. The whole team has to pull together. I'd been captain for a couple of years before George came to the club, but we needed eleven captains out there on the pitch. With George around, everybody soon started to play better.

"It's always a sign of a good team when there's plenty of talking and shouting going on between the players. We all have to know what's going on if we're going to play as a team.

"From the day George arrived, things started to get

> I was pleased with the way things went for me at the World Cup. It would have been even better if my goal against Argentina had stood.

more organised. I certainly felt I was getting more help with the defensive duties from the whole team.

"A good defence starts with the forwards, moves through the midfield to the back four and the keeper. It's much better when the whole team's doing the job properly."

The rewards came quickly for Spurs under the George Graham regime. They reached the Worthington Cup Final where Campbell captained them to a dramatic last-minute

victory over Leicester City.

"That was a very special day for me and the club," says Sol. "I'd played at Wembley many times for England but it was different playing there for Tottenham.

"The place has a magic all of its own. Ever since I was a little boy, I've always wanted to play there.

"When I was a kid I didn't think about anything else besides football. I was always out kicking a ball or watching a game somewhere. I never used to stick in one position when I was at school. In those days I didn't really know where I wanted to play.

"It's only since I've been in the Tottenham first team that I've settled into my best position at centre-back. That doesn't mean to say I don't like getting forward and trying to score a few goals whenever I can.

"At the start of last season I even found myself Tottenham's leading scorer for quite a while. That was a very funny kind of position for me to be in because I'd only ever scored two league goals before then.

"Suddenly they were going in every time I went up for a free-kick or corner. But I never ignore my main responsibilities.

"It's good if you can get forward and be productive for the team but first and foremost I'm a defender. That's what the club pays me to do and the manager certainly won't let me forget it." ■

T was at the World Cup in France in 1998 that Sol really came good at the highest international level. He was a rock in England's back four and even thought he'd scored the goal to take the team into the quarter-finals only to see it ruled out for a foul by Alan Shearer.

"The World Cup showed me the ultimate stage on which I could prove myself as a player," says Sol. "It doesn't come any bigger than that.

"Every game you play is vital in World Cups and European Championship Finals. No player wants to miss out on such important matches.

"The World Cup is the opportunity to play against the very best in the game. Everybody wants to be able to play well and express themselves in that sort of arena.

"I was pleased with the way things went for me at the World Cup. It would have been even better if my goal against Argentina had stood.

"I think my best is still to come at that level. When the next World Cup comes around in 2002 I'll only be 27 and that should mean I'm approaching my best.

"At the moment I'm still only a young man in football terms. If I go to Korea and Japan with England in a couple of years time, I should be a much more mature player by then." ■

TONY DORIGO is enjoying life to the

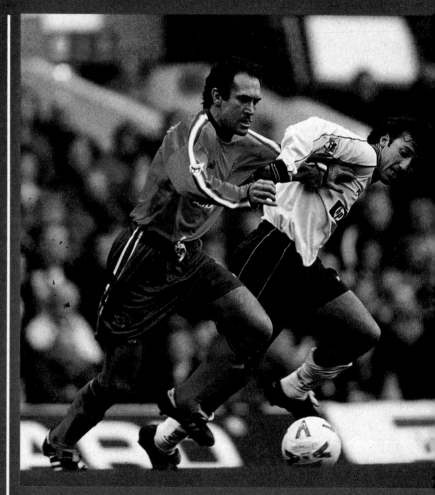

NSTANCES of England players fluffing spot-kicks in penalty shoot-outs have become depressingly commonplace. It is now almost expected. After a few spontaneous tears, men like Stuart Pearce, Chris Waddle, Gareth Southgate, David Batty and Paul Ince have been forgiven and allowed to get on with the rest of their careers. Tony Dorigo expected similar treatment when he was the guilty party at the end of Torino's Italian Serie B promotion play-off game with Perugia two seasons ago. He didn't realise how wrong he was.

Unable to support another high budget attempt to get back into the top division, the Turin side decided to cut their losses and, halfway through his two-year contract, they gave Dorigo an ultimatum - take a 50 per cent cut in wages or don't bother coming back.

The former Chelsea, Aston Villa and Leeds player decided on the latter, but not before engaging in a long and intense legal battle in order to gain a satisfactory settlement on his contract.

Finally he was able to switch his thoughts back to football and a return to the English Premiership.

Despite the season being already well under way, he had no problems fixing himself up as Jim Smith took him to Derby County.

As he reveals, the Rams boss also saved him from going mad.

Says the Australian-born defender, "It got quite messy with Torino in the end but I was determined to make sure I got what I was owed. I was the injured party in all of it.

"I didn't particularly like going to the courts but it turned out to be the

only way. The big problem was that Italian law is so different from its English equivalent. Quite apart from it being in a different language, it is very technical and hard to comprehend.

"I had hoped to have everything sorted out quickly so I could link up with someone for pre-season training. Unfortunately, just as we'd sorted our case out, we were told that the Italian courts were shut for seven weeks for a holiday!

"So if there are any bank

robbers out there, remember to go to Italy in late summer because there will be nobody to convict you!

"That left me in limbo. I couldn't join another club and was having to keep fit on my own. At the same time I was in constant contact with a host of different solicitors.

"It was a horrible time. It became so bad that I even took up fishing. I'd never had any inclination to try it before and even used to take the mickey out of former team mates who enjoyed it. I had a lot of time

winner!

full at Pride park

on my hands, though, gave it a whirl and, in the end, turned out to be pretty good at it.

"Thank God Jim Smith stepped in when he did. He saved my sanity!

"Having said that, Italy was still a brilliant experience and if I'd had my way, I'd have stayed there at least until the end of my Torino contract. I'm certain that if I stay in the game after retiring and look at becoming a coach or manager, that year in Italy will prove to be vital.

"Before I went over there, I thought the Italians spent all their time working on ball skills. That proved to be far from the case.

"They concentrate on fitness in a big way and I probably came to Derby fitter than I'd ever been.

"The technical organisation had to be seen to be believed. Every part of the game was broken down into the minutest detail.

"Every club was well drilled and that made it difficult for Torino. It was a bit like the situation Manchester City found themselves in when they were relegated to the Second Division a couple of years back. We were the big fish and were there to be shot at.

"We finished in the last promotion place but level on points with Perugia. Goal difference didn't come into play so we were forced into a play-off. Having had a man sent off early on and been a goal behind, we managed to equalise to force extra time and penalties.

"I'm usually pretty reliable at taking spot-kicks and have taken a few since joining Derby, but in that game I hit mine against the inside of the post and missed.

"Even then I had no inkling that it was to be my last game for the club. I was made man of the match and was the club's Player of the

Year. I left for a summer holiday back in England with everyone determined to win promotion automatically the next time. Everything seemed fine.

"It was only when my tickets back out to Italy after the summer break failed to turn up that I realised something wasn't quite right.

"I wanted to return - who wouldn't? The lifestyle I enjoyed out there was something else.

"I lived in a barn conversion in the hills, overlooking the Alps. It had marble floors and 17th century furniture. You can live with those sorts of things.

"I always intended to come back and, although it came about a bit earlier than I expected or hoped, I'm delighted to be in the Premiership with Derby County.

"People have short memories and when I left England I wondered if I'd be remembered. Fortunately Jim Smith hadn't forgotten.

"I landed on my feet with Derby. Jim Smith is one of the few great coaches around and, as I want to go into management when I retire, I've been able to play as well as take notes for future reference."

Although out of English football for only a year, Dorigo, capped 15 times under England managers Bobby Robson and Graham Taylor, noticed a big difference on arriving at Pride Park. For him, it was a change for the better.

"Wing back systems are now the

> **"Thank God Jim Smith stepped in when he did. He saved my sanity!"**

norm," he goes on. "That wasn't the case when I left for Italy.

"The influx of foreign coaches and players has had an effect and the game seems to be coming round to a more continental style of play. The pace is still quicker than in Italy, but there are now definite similarities.

"It suits me down to the ground because I've always enjoyed getting forward and I think I'm a decent crosser of a ball. The system seems made for me." ■

a glass act!

How an on-loan keeper became the toast of Carlisle!

T was the stuff dreams are made of! To score the goal that saved your team from the ultimate indignity of dropping out of the Football League... especially when the goal is scored by a GOALIE in the dying seconds of the last game of the season!!

Carlisle United were staring relegation in the face. The score was one-all against Plymouth. With fellow-strugglers Scarborough also drawing, the Brunton Park side knew only a win would do. A draw would see them head out of the league for the first time in 71 years. Then came the moment of drama. With the referee looking at his watch, Carlisle forced a corner.

Up came on-loan keeper Jimmy Glass to add some weight to the attack. A header was well saved by Plymouth goalie James Dungey. The ball fell to the unmarked Glass and...well, the rest is history!

The Cumbrian crowd mobbed their unlikely hero as they celebrated their great escape.

Glass was modest about his achievement, but Carlisle chairman Michael Knighton, who once came close to buying Manchester United, was more enthusiastic about his hero keeper, and joked about erecting a giant statue of Glass behind the goal where he scored!

Sadly, Carlisle fans didn't get the chance to cheer Glass this season. He returned to his club, Swindon, after the loan period ended.

nick **WRIGHT** Watford

TOPICAL TIMES FOOTBALL BOOK

the only way

STEVE HAYWARD was one of the few players to survive the Kevin Keegan whirlwind that swept through Craven Cottage. The former Derby County player was there when Keegan arrived at Fulham and still there when he left to take over as England boss.

Like all the Fulham players, Hayward knows exactly what Keegan did for his career. Not that his ambitions ended with the manager's departure.

"It's everybody's dream to play in the Premiership," says Steve. "Who knows, it could happen very soon at this club.

"So far in my career I've won the Auto-Windscreens Shield, a couple of Division Three medals and last season's Division Two Championship. Now I'm looking at bigger things.

"At 28, I've been around in the game for quite a while. But I don't think it's unrealistic to be thinking about playing in the Premiership.

"I might be a late starter, but if you give up on your dreams what's the point of going on? You never know what's around the corner in football.

"Kevin Keegan definitely made me a better player. In his first year in charge a lot of players left the club but he gave me the chance to stay and prove what I could do.

"He made me express myself more as a player. Suddenly, I felt much more confident out there on the pitch.

> " **It's everybody's dream to play in the Premiership,"** says Steve. **"Who knows, it could happen very soon at this club.** "

"Kevin lets you know that you're the best and we went out to prove just that. There's nobody better at instilling confidence in players.

"If he had something to say he'd say it, but he certainly had no axe to grind. He's a manager who wears his heart on his sleeve and that's what players want.

"Of course, he didn't have to keep me at the club. He could quite easily have gone out and bought somebody else.

"There was actually a time early last season when it looked like I might be leaving the club. I'm very glad that didn't happen.

"When Kevin first took the England job on a part-time basis, it could have gone badly wrong for us. Instead, we found our best form of the season and put a great run of results together to clinch the Championship.

"There was always something happening at Fulham last season with Kevin and Mr Al Fayed around. One day, Michael Jackson came to watch a match at Craven Cottage. I was half expecting Elvis to turn up after that!

"But the most important thing here at Fulham has been football. That's why everybody will be busting a gut to get promoted again this season." ■

44

is up!

STEVE HAYWARD

stephen GLASS Newcastle Utd

jonathan GOULD Celtic

TOPICAL TIMES FOOTBALL BOOK

a century of soccer

no3. 1940-49 1950-59

Player of the decade: Tommy Lawton

Photos: Hulton Getty

WHEN Tommy Lawton was first called up to play for England at the age of 19, he swaggered into the Everton dressing room as though he had just won the World Cup single-handedly.

Old pro Dixie Dean, who had banged a few goals for England himself, was not impressed, and promptly threw him into the bath to cool off.

The dousing did nothing to quench the youngster's spirit, however. During his debut in Cardiff, England were awarded a penalty and Lawton was asked to take it. He promptly slammed it into the back of the net to become his country's youngest-ever goalscorer, a title he would keep until the appearance of a certain Michael Owen last year.

His side lost 4-2 that day, but Lawton went on to become one of England's best-ever goalscorers, notching 22 goals in 23 official appearances. But if you count his 28 strikes in 29 unofficial internationals played during the Second World War, which robbed him of huge potential achievement, he can be classed as England's all-time leading scorer.

He is also the youngest player to score a hat-trick, aged 17 years and 4 days. He couldn't have picked a better occasion either-it was his debut for Burnley in 1936.

A legendary header of the ball, he began his six-club career at Turf Moor where he developed his aerial prowess by heading a ball tied to a rope underneath the stand.

Following spells with Everton and Chelsea, he shocked the football world by moving to Third Division Notts County at the height of his career in 1947, thereby sabotaging his international career.

He had promised to help out an old friend, Arthur Strolley, who had just taken over as manager at Meadow Lane, and refused to break his word.

However, he later moved to Brentford and finished his career back at the top with Arsenal.

Other leading players of the 1940s:

WILF MANNION. Football's first rebel. Middlesbrough's star player went on strike over a contract dispute, and took a job as a salesman until he won his case.

JOHNNY CAREY. Irish-born full-back who served Manchester United for 15 years and, as team captain, led them to League and FA Cup victories.

DENIS COMPTON. One of sport's great all-rounders and the first sporting hero to

advertise non-sporting goods. The Arsenal winger also batted for Middlesex and England at cricket, and became a pin-up when advertising Brylcreem.

RAICH CARTER. Carter was the youngest player to lift the League Championship, with Sunderland in 1936. After the war he moved to Derby County in a £8,000 deal, winning the FA Cup in his first season.

Milestones:

1946. Football moves into full swing again after the interruption of the war years, and Britain rejoins FIFA.

1947. Great Britain beat the Rest of Europe 6-1 in Glasgow.

1949. Stanley Rous, secretary of the Football Association, is knighted.

WEMBLEY has staged its share of memorable and dramatic finals. Few have stood out quite so much as the 1953 FA Cup Final. No others have been identified by the name of one player. But this will always be known as The Matthews Final.

With only 20 minutes remaining, Blackpool trailed Bolton Wanderers 3-1 and appeared down and out. The oldest player on the pitch, 38-year-old Stanley Matthews, seemed destined to collect his third runners-up medal in five years.

But the Wizard of the Dribble was not finished. Matthews began to destroy Bolton with a series of blistering runs and crosses. He created three goals as Blackpool completed an incredible comeback to win 4-3.

Team-mate Stan Mortensen claimed a hat-trick that day, but the final belonged to Matthews.

It is perhaps fitting that the occasion of an FA Cup Final should be indelibly stamped with the mark of a player who has been acclaimed as England's finest-ever footballer.

His career, which began in 1933 with his hometown club, Stoke City, continued for an amazing 32 years before he finally retired at the age of 50, having returned to Stoke.

He was Footballer of the Year in 1948 and 1963 and won the first-ever European Footballer of the Year award in 1956. He also won 64 England caps in an international career which spanned 23 years and was knighted in 1965. ■

Photos: Hulton Getty

Player of the decade: Sir Stanley Mathews

Other leading players of the 1950s:

TOM FINNEY. Now Sir Tom, he was affectionately known in his playing days as The Preston Plumber, which was his trade. A devastating winger, he won 76 caps for England, was Footballer of the Year twice and scored a record 187 goals in 433 League appearances for Preston North End.

NAT LOFTHOUSE. Achieved the remarkable record of 30 goals in 33 appearances for England, and was his country's record scorer when he retired. One famous goal, when he ran the length of the pitch to score the winner in a 3-2 away victory over Austria in 1952, earned him his nickname, 'The Lion of Vienna.' Footballer of the Year in 1953, he also collected an FA Cup winner's medal in 1958 with Bolton.

DUNCAN EDWARDS. The youngest player ever to play for Manchester United. When he died with seven other members of The Busby Babes in the 1958 Munich Air Disaster at the age of only 21, he had already won 18 England caps and two Championship medals. Described by Matt Busby at the time as, "The most complete player in Britain."

BILLY WRIGHT. Wright became the first player to win 100 England caps, eventually totalling 105. 90 of these were as captain. He skippered Wolves to three League titles in 1954, 1958 and 1959.

Milestones:

1950. A world record crowd of 203,500 watch the World Cup Final between Brazil and Uruguay in Rio de Janeiro.

1952. Newcastle become the first club to win the FA Cup in successive seasons this century.

1953. Previously unbeaten at home, England are brought down to earth, losing 6-3 to Hungary at Wembley. Worse comes year later when they lose 7-1 in Budapest.

1956. Real Madrid win the first European Cup.

49

1 TONY ALEXANDER ADAMS was born in Romford, Essex, on October 10th, 1966. His father, Alex, had been on the books of West Ham as a centre half. It was Alex who would prove to be the first and most significant influence on Tony's career.

2 When Tony's dad stopped playing, he formed the Sunday morning boys team Dagenham United and it was there that Tony assumed an early winning habit. United, with Tony in the heart of defence, were unbeaten in the five years they were in existence and won the Essex Cup every year during that time.

3 Tony played trial games for London sides West Ham, Orient and Fulham as well as attracting interest from Manchester United, but it was for Terry Neill's Arsenal...starring Liam Brady... that Tony signed schoolboy forms in November 1980. Tony's first defensive partner in the Gunners' youth team was Martin Keown, now a stalwart alongside Adams in the current Highbury first team.

top

4 Tony played his first match for the first team versus Sunderland on 5th November, 1983, becoming the second-youngest player in Arsenal's history to make his debut.

5 It was the arrival of George Graham as manager in May 1986, that saw Tony's career really take off. The ex-Arsenal star handed Tony the club captaincy at the age of 20, and in the ensuing years saw two League Cups, one FA Cup, two League Championships and a Cup-Winners' Cup finish up in the Highbury trophy room.

gunner
The story of TONY ADAMS

6 By now, Tony was an England regular, having made his debut against Spain in February, 1987, when Gary Lineker scored all four goals in a 4-2 England win. During the reign of Terry Venables, Tony captained his country on thirteen occasions, including England's run in Euro 96. His record as skipper was Won 5, Drawn 7 and Lost 1.

7 After the departure of George Graham, Bruce Rioch and Stewart Houston took the Arsenal managerial reins briefly, before Arsene Wenger was appointed in September, 1996. Before long, the glory days were back at Highbury when the League and FA Cup Double was done in 1998.

8 An ankle injury earlier that year saw Tony spend 30 days recuperating in the south of France. He returned fit and fresh, ready to play a vital role in the Double and in England's World Cup campaign in France.

9 Despite the leadership qualities of Adams, Arsenal failed to emulate their achievements of season 1997-98, being pipped for the Premiership title by Manchester United and losing to the Old Trafford side in the FA Cup semi-final.

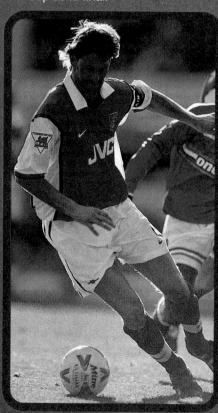

● **But you can bet that with Tony Adams in their side, Arsenal will be Gunning for Glory again this season!**

...and mother makes four!

a WELSH woman took to heart the old cliche, "If you can't beat 'em, join 'em" when she followed in the footsteps of her husband and two sons to qualify as a football referee.

Sharon Duddridge felt left out when husband Steve and sons, 14-year-old Stephen and 11-year-old Stuart, spent their weekends eating and sleeping the game.

On a typical weekend, Steve would coach a side in the Gwent Junior League and the two boys would play for organised teams.

The family would sit down to watch Match of the Day on Saturday evening and argue about decisions. It left the 37-year-old school caterer from Newport feeling exasperated.

"When I tried to raise a point, I was often told that I didn't know what I was talking about," said Sharon. "Then, earlier this year, Steve and Stephen passed their referee exams. As a joke, I suggested that Stuart and myself might as well take them, too.

"Steve left me speechless when he came back with application forms. I decided there was nothing to lose and took the course.

"There was a lot to learn, ranging from the offside rule to the weight of the ball. But after a few weeks of studying I also passed my exams.

"I think the rest of the family were quite proud of me. It showed that I wasn't one of those football-hating women."

Sharon's first game in charge after qualifying was to referee a local school match with Steve and Stuart acting as assistant referees, while Stephen was playing.

She added, "The television cameras were at the game because it was such a novelty. I certainly don't know of any other instance where a mother, father and two sons were all involved in the same match especially when the mother was the referee!

"Now I can prove I am talking sense when commenting on incidents on Match of the Day.

"If anybody tells me to 'put your specs on' or says that I am 'only a woman', I will show them the red card!" ■

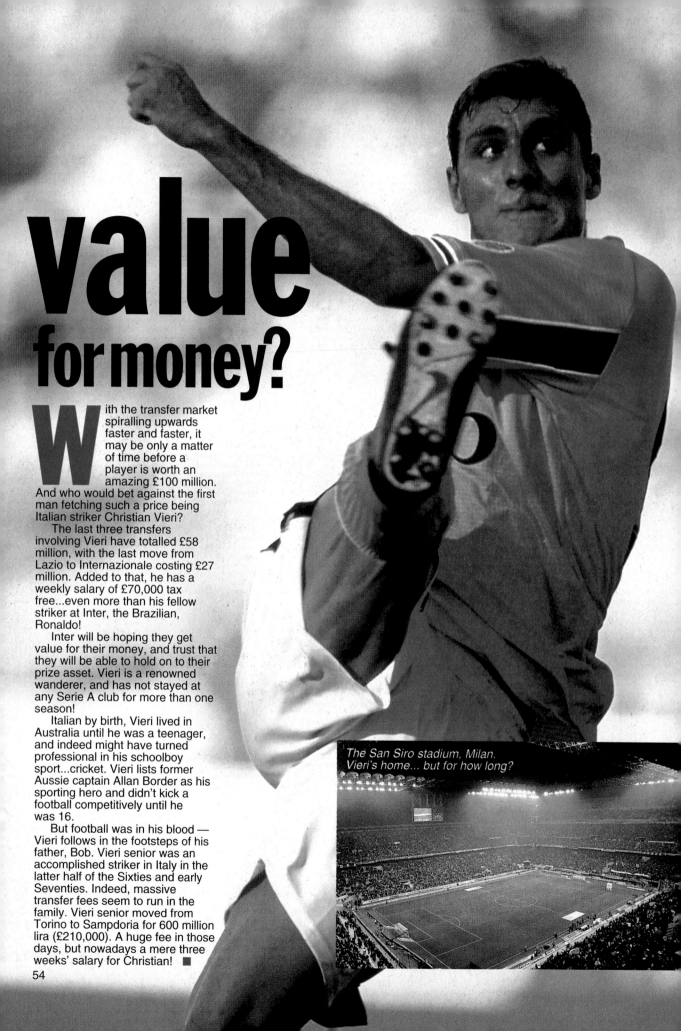

value
for money?

With the transfer market spiralling upwards faster and faster, it may be only a matter of time before a player is worth an amazing £100 million. And who would bet against the first man fetching such a price being Italian striker Christian Vieri?

The last three transfers involving Vieri have totalled £58 million, with the last move from Lazio to Internazionale costing £27 million. Added to that, he has a weekly salary of £70,000 tax free...even more than his fellow striker at Inter, the Brazilian, Ronaldo!

Inter will be hoping they get value for their money, and trust that they will be able to hold on to their prize asset. Vieri is a renowned wanderer, and has not stayed at any Serie A club for more than one season!

Italian by birth, Vieri lived in Australia until he was a teenager, and indeed might have turned professional in his schoolboy sport...cricket. Vieri lists former Aussie captain Allan Border as his sporting hero and didn't kick a football competitively until he was 16.

But football was in his blood — Vieri follows in the footsteps of his father, Bob. Vieri senior was an accomplished striker in Italy in the latter half of the Sixties and early Seventies. Indeed, massive transfer fees seem to run in the family. Vieri senior moved from Torino to Sampdoria for 600 million lira (£210,000). A huge fee in those days, but nowadays a mere three weeks' salary for Christian! ∎

The San Siro stadium, Milan. Vieri's home... but for how long?

robbie **SAVAGE** Leicester City

TOPICAL TIMES FOOTBALL BOOK

seeing treble!

Same man.... different trophies!

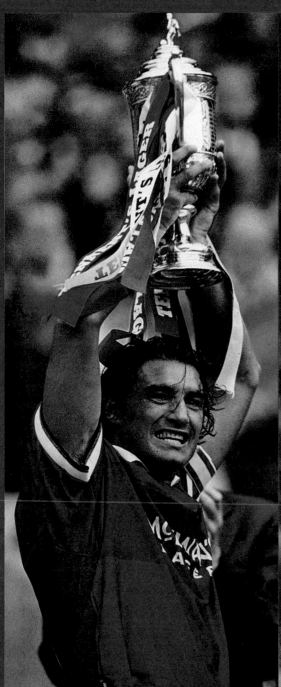

Trophy-less in his first season with Rangers, Lorenzo Amoruso more than made up for it last season when he captained Rangers to the Scottish League, Scottish Cup and Scottish League Cup "treble".

WORLDWIDE ambassador for football, mere mention of Sir Bobby Charlton's name is still guaranteed to spark recognition around the globe.

The consummate gentleman, both on and off the field, Bobby was central to the great rebuilding of Manchester United following the Munich Air Disaster in 1958 which destroyed the Busby Babes.

Bobby, himself one of the Babes, survived the plane crash at the age of 20, and as manager Matt Busby set about reviving his dream of creating a team to conquer Europe, he built his new side around the talents of Charlton.

A brilliant attacking player, Charlton was noted for his pace, accurate long-range passing and powerful shooting. It was fitting that, when United finally won the European Cup in 1968, skipper Charlton scored two of the goals in the 4-1 defeat of Benfica in the Wembley final.

Together with George Best and Denis Law, Bobby's name became synonymous with United's great team of the 1960s which had swept all before them on the way to that great triumph. After winning three League Championships and an FA Cup, that night at Wembley was his crowning glory with United.

His greatest moment in an England jersey had come two years earlier when he starred in Sir Alf Ramsey's side which lifted the World Cup, also at Wembley. Throughout the tournament, Charlton's goals and all-pervading influence carried England along, helped by the wave of national fervour which gripped the nation. In the Final against West Germany, he and his great rival, Franz Beckenbauer, came head-to-head, with Charlton running out the victor as England triumphed 4-2 after extra time.

Four years later, Charlton's international career ended as the Germans exacted revenge by knocking England out of the World Cup in Mexico at the quarter-final stage. But his international goal tally of 49 remains an England record.

In 1972, Charlton left Manchester United to become manager of Preston North End. It was an unsuccessful attempt and he retired from the game two years later. However, he has remained involved with football as a director of Manchester United. He was awarded his knighthood in 1994. ■

58

topical times

a century of soccer

no4. 1960-69

Player of the decade: Bobby Charlton

Photo: Hulton Getty

Other leading players of the 1960s

Photo: Hulton Getty

GEORGE BEST. Irish genius, hailed as the most talented footballer of his generation. Known as the fifth Beatle, his extrovert style made him the personification of the 1960s.

BILLY McNEILL. Captain of the great Celtic side of the 1960s, who became the first British team to win the European Cup, in 1967. Nine Scottish Champions' medals and seven Scottish Cups. 29 caps for Scotland.

BOBBY MOORE. Captain of the England side which won the World Cup. Immaculate defender who also led West Ham United to Cup Winners' Cup glory in 1965.

Milestones

1960 Launch of the Football League Cup.

1961 Maximum wage is abolished. Johnny Haynes of Fulham becomes the first £100 per week footballer.

1964 Rangers make a clean sweep of Scottish League, Scottish Cup and League Cup.

1965 Stanley Matthews is knighted in his farewell season.

don't mention

bolton's Eidur Gudjohnsen has crammed more into three years than most footballers can manage in a whole career. The Icelandic striker made his mark as a 20-year-old at Bolton Wanderers last season, but his performances for the Reebok Stadium side were hardly a surprise considering his previous billing as Ronaldo's strike partner!

Yes, that is THE Ronaldo. The Brazilian superstar who is rated by many as the best footballer on the planet.

The unusual Iceland-Brazil strike-force was formed at Dutch club, PSV Eindhoven, in 1996. Although Gudjohnsen was only 17 at the time and Ronaldo 19, the pair looked set for a bright future.

However, while the Brazilian climbed an upward spiral by moving on to Barcelona and Inter, Gudjohnsen's progress shuddered to a halt when he suffered a career-threatening injury.

While Ronaldo terrorised the defences of Juventus, Lazio and Parma, Eidur fought to regain his fitness at Bolton. The powerful striker is now ready to pick up where he left off.

Says Eidur, "Things were going well for me at PSV, and I had just completed my first season in Eindhoven and had played eight times for the first team when disaster struck.

"I was finding my feet at the club and was confident about the future. Then I was selected to play for Iceland's Under-18s against the Republic of Ireland in Dublin, and that's where my problems began.

"I can still remember it vividly. It was May 1996 and I broke my fibula and tore all the ligaments in my ankle. It was a very bad injury. Within two days, I had flown back to Holland and had the operation to fix my leg.

"The surgeons told me that I would be fit within four or five months, but it took much longer than that. There were complications and I suffered bad tendonitis. All in all, I was out for two years.

"I didn't play for PSV again. When my contract expired in the summer of 1998, they did not offer me a new deal. The club doctors said that I couldn't recover from such a bad injury, but I always believed that I would.

"I was very disappointed for two years when I was trying to get fit, but I was just as upset when I found out that PSV weren't going to give me the chance to prove myself.

"In a way, I wasn't really bothered that they let me go because I wasn't sure that I wanted to stay there anyway. If they didn't think I was going to play again, there was no point in staying.

"I'm just glad that things have started to go in my favour again. Signing for Bolton last season gave me the opportunity that I was looking for and I know I can rediscover my best form."

By a strange twist of fate, though, his career was relaunched by a trip to Dublin, the city where it all began to go so wrong for him two years earlier.

Eidur continues, "At the end of my contract at PSV, I went back to Iceland. I just said to myself that I wanted to go home.

"My girlfriend was expecting a baby at the time, so I wanted to relax a

Eidur missed a couple of chances for Bolton...

...and don't mention

Bolton's dreams of a return to the Premiership were dashed by Graham Taylor's Watford in the Division One play-off Final at Wembley.

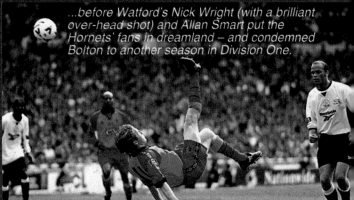

...before Watford's Nick Wright (with a brilliant over-head shot) and Allan Smart put the Hornets' fans in dreamland – and condemned Bolton to another season in Division One.

dublin!

Eidur Gudjohnsen

bit and overcome my injury. I felt that going home was the best thing for everybody.

"I put on a lot of weight, though, and I wasn't in any shape to play football. Fortunately, I managed to play a few games for KR Reykjavik and that allowed me to get my appetite back and regain my fitness.

"After a handful of games for Reykjavik, Bolton invited me over for a trial during their summer tour of Ireland. Manager Colin Todd had heard of my reputation as a good player at PSV and he decided to take a chance on me.

"I had to fly into Dublin, however, and meet up with the team. I obviously have some bad memories of Dublin and they all came flooding back to me when I arrived.

"I had only been back for a matter of minutes when I discovered that the airport had lost all of my luggage! When that happened, I thought 'Here we go again!'

"I was in the same airport as last time, walking through the same terminal. I couldn't help but think that things were going to go wrong again. Luckily, that didn't happen and I have no problems with Ireland now.

"Bolton liked what they saw and they offered me a contract. I was delighted to get back at such a high level and I hope that Bolton see the best of me because there is plenty still to come.

"I have a lot to prove. I am still very young and I believe I have another 12 or 15 years in football." ■

the play-offs!

Triumph for Smart and Wright...

...Misery for Eidur Gudjohnsen!

the northern line

One-way ticket to Middlesbrough please, says DEAN GORDON

DEAN GORDON surveyed the wreckage of his final eighteen months at Crystal Palace, and realised that the time had come for him to leave Selhurst Park, and London, for the good of his career.

The capital city may have become the fashionable place to play football in recent seasons, but Gordon knew he had to test himself on and off the pitch in order to rediscover his best form. Leaving London was part of the challenge.

The former England Under-21 full-back had seen his career stall after a troublesome Achilles injury. Nobody needed to tell the 26-year-old that he was treading water at relegated Palace.

A £900,000 transfer to Middlesbrough in the summer of 1998 rescued Gordon from a return to the First Division. Dean had to leave his home city behind, but he purposefully moved to the north-east to kick-start his career.

Dean says: "A lot of players are moving to London nowadays, but I took the opposite route and moved away. I was desperate for a fresh start and needed to find out for myself whether I could do it again after my injury.

"Before I tore my Achilles I was really sharp and playing well, but 18 months after coming back, I still wasn't playing well and hadn't found my best form.

"I needed a new start to get the best out of me and was hoping that a new challenge would spark me back into life.

"Considering that Bryan Robson, Viv Anderson, Paul Gascoigne and Paul Merson were at Middlesbrough at the

> **"I like a challenge and coming to Middlesbrough was definitely a challenge for a born and bred London boy".**

time, I was really looking forward to moving here.

"I knew that playing among such good coaches and players would either make me or break me.

"Leaving Palace was more than just a football move. My mum and all my friends still live in London, but I was just beginning to feel that life was too hectic down there. I wanted a break from the place.

"I like a challenge and coming to Middlesbrough was definitely a challenge for a born and bred London boy.

"I'm so happy I decided to come here. A lot of people have slaughtered the place in the past, saying it's not a nice area to live, but I like it. It's not like London, it's more relaxed, but that is helping me because I can concentrate on my football more."

Dean adds, "My final season at Palace didn't go well for me. I was still trying to overcome my injury which had kept me out for nine months the previous season.

"That set me back more than I ever imagined. I thought I could work my way back after a few weeks, but it didn't work like that. I made a few mistakes, like coming back too early, and it showed on the pitch.

"I wasn't fit enough or sharp enough and I was caught out. I wanted to be thrown in at the deep end at the time, but I should have been more patient.

"The takeover at Palace also dragged on and it affected morale at the club. It was impossible to concentrate on the football. Middlesbrough threw me a lifeline when they bought me.

"When I first arrived at Boro,

we all changed in portakabins before our new training ground was finished, but I enjoyed that because it was all a change from Palace. Everything is different here and it is making me a better player.

"When I looked around the dressing-room, the thought of playing with Gazza, Gary Pallister and Andy Townsend was daunting. I was quite nervous early on.

"I knew I had to earn the respect of my new team-mates, but I was still playing the Crystal Palace way, so I had to adapt to my new surroundings quickly.

"Boro are more of a passing team than Palace, but I was still looking to hit the ball long. I quickly began to pass the ball around lot more. I have learned so much in the time I have been at Middlesbrough.

"I am very happy here and that is showing in my football. I just love going to training and the whole environment here. I even skip breakfast at home now because I can have bacon and eggs at the training ground with the lads.

"After a couple of bad years at Palace, it is great to be enjoying my football at Middlesbrough. If it was a make or break move, it hasn't broken me yet." ∎

keith **GILLESPIE** Blackburn Rovers

dion **DUBLIN** Aston Villa

TOPICAL TIMES FOOTBALL BOOK

tony cottee

Leicester City's Tony Cottee is one of the most instinctive and consistent strikers in the Premiership. In his career with West Ham United (twice), Everton and Leicester he has scored over 250 times, and in April, 1999, joined a handful of players who have scored 200 league goals. So when we asked him to pick his favourite ten, he had lots to choose from!

West Ham Utd 3, Tottenham 0. First Division, January 1st, 1983.

It was New Year's Day and my full debut for West Ham at Upton Park against our London rivals Tottenham. I scored after 25 minutes when a free-kick by Geoff Pike was headed towards goal by Joe Gallagher. Spurs keeper Ray Clemence tipped the ball onto the bar, but as it bounced down I put it into the net.

Not the most fantastic goal I ever scored, but as a 17-year-old it was a wonderful moment to score my first-ever goal for West Ham in front of over 33,000 people.

West Ham Utd 3, Nottingham Forest 2. First Division, 21st November, 1987.

This was the best technical goal I have ever scored. I had scored earlier in the game, but the second is the one that stands out. Mark Ward crossed to me in the penalty area, but it arrived at an awkward height. Ten yards from goal, I couldn't volley it or head it, so I opted to go for an overhead kick.. Luckily, I caught the ball perfectly and it flew straight past Forest goalkeeper Steve Sutton into the top corner.

3 Everton 4, Newcastle Utd 0. First Division, August 27th, 1988.
Another debut goal, this time for Everton. I had just signed for the club in a British record transfer, costing £2.2 million from West Ham, so to score after just 34 seconds was a dream start. Graeme Sharp received a long ball from Neil McDonald and went for goal. Newcastle `keeper Dave Beasant couldn`t hold onto the ball and I nipped in to net the rebound from 12 yards. There was a lot of pressure on me that day, but I went on to grab a hat-trick. It was a wonderful way to kick off my Everton career.

4 Everton 1, Tottenham 0. First Division, December 3rd, 1988.
This was my 100th League goal and I have chosen it because of the significance of reaching that landmark. I latched onto an Ian Snodin pass, beat the off-side trap and took the ball on my chest.I took a touch and hit the ball across the face of the goal, beating Bobby Mimms at the Gwladys Street End.

5 Everton 3, Nottingham Forest 4. Simod Cup Final (Wembley), April 30th, 1989.
Despite finishing the game with a runners-up medal, I have chosen this goal because it was my first at Wembley. It was back in the days when I had a bit of pace! Trevor Steven knocked a ball over the Forest defence and I outpaced my marker, Des Walker, before controlling the ball on my thigh and knocking it through the legs of goalkeeper Steve Sutton.

6 Everton 4, Liverpool 4. FA Cup Fifth Round replay, February 20th, 1991.
I was on the bench for this game, but with Everton trailing 3-2 with five minutes to go, manager Howard Kendall opted to throw me on. I was wondering what on earth I could do in five minutes. In the 89th minute, however, Stuart McCall flicked the ball into my path and I read the ball quicker than anybody else. I looked up and placed a left-foot curler past Bruce Grobbelaar to take the game into extra-time, when I notched a second goal.

7 Sheffield Wednesday 3, Everton 1. Premiership, February 6th, 1993.
When I talk about this goal, nobody believes me because it is the type I am not noted for scoring. I received the ball on the halfway line and turned my marker. The opposition half opened up in front of me as I went past two more Wednesday defenders. Thirty yards from goal, I spotted keeper Chris Woods off his line. I chipped him from way out and it floated into the net. We were 3-0 down at the time, so it was only a consolation.
Funnily enough, the goal came second in the BBC's Goal of the Month competition. It is the only time I have made the top ten!

8

Manchester United 0, Leicester City 1. Premiership, January 31st, 1998.

This was a big goal for me for a number of reasons. Old Trafford had been a bogey ground for me and I had waited 15 years to get my first goal there. It came 30 minutes into the game. I latched on to a Garry Parker through ball after United defender Henning Berg missed the ball. When the ball broke free, I put it past Peter Schmeichel to seal a 1-0 win.

I had only just returned to England after an unhappy spell in Malaysia. That goal at Old Trafford relaunched my career and put me back in the public eye. It was a great day.

9

● Leicester City 1, Sunderland 1. Worthington Cup Semi-Final, second leg, February 17th, 1999.

This wasn't the most fantastic goal I have ever scored, but in terms of importance it is one of my favourite strikes. We were trailing 1-0 on the night until Robbie Savage passed to Neil Lennon on the right. Neil found me in the box and I ran into space and caught the ball flush on the volley to lift it over Thomas Sorensen in the Sunderland goal. I scored twice in the first leg, but this goal was the clincher and took Leicester to Wembley. It was a very significant goal.

10

Tottenham Hotspur 0, Leicester City 2. Premiership, April 3rd, 1999.

This was the goal I had been waiting for...my 200th League goal. I headed a throw-in into the path of Emile Heskey and he homed in on goal. I was knocked to the ground by a Spurs defender, but I picked myself up as Emile was running into the box. He squared the ball and I scored from about four yards. It was a typical Cottee goal!

It was perhaps fate that I would notch my 200th League goal against Spurs as my 1st and 100th had also came against them.

A couple of days later, Leicester City presented me with a glass decanter to mark my achievement.

stuart McCALL Bradford City

TOPICAL TIMES FOOTBALL BOOK

patriot gam

Rangers' COLIN HENDRY will give his all for club and country!

AFTER LEADING Blackburn Rovers to the English title in 1995, and epitomising the Scottish 'Braveheart' image as his country battled their way to the Finals of Euro '96 and France '98, Colin Hendry is now one of British football's best-known faces.

These days, starring at the heart of Dick Advocaat's multi-millionaire Glasgow Rangers, Hendry's profile certainly hasn't diminished - but Colin reckons medals beat fame any day.

Despite his high profile and financial fortune, Hendry's 16 years in the game haven't produced too many medals or trophies, and he was one of the most delighted men at Celtic Park when Rangers beat St Johnstone to lift the League Cup just a few months into his Ibrox career.

With a four-year contract in his pocket, Colin knew there was more than an even chance of adding many more medals to his small collection - but he knows it will only be possible if he maintains his hunger.

"It's great to be with a club who can play in Europe every season and win some, if not all, the domestic honours available," 33-year-old Hendry enthuses.

"To be honest, I haven't won too many trophies during my time in the game and believe me, it's not

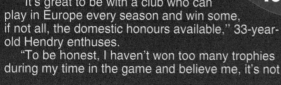

something you take for granted once you win your first!

"But no club can guarantee you anything, and we have already seen Celtic start to spend big and improve their squad to provide us with some stiff competition.

"Obviously, there is a lot of cash for the manager of Rangers, and the whole set-up - the stadium, the season-ticket sales, and the history of the club - is all geared towards success.

"You still have to get the right blend of players, though, no matter how much money you spend, and that's one reason I don't believe a club like ours should ever be filled entirely with non-Scots.

"We have great players from all over the world, but I hope there is always space for young Scots like the ones who had a chance last season - Barry Ferguson, Barry Nicholson, Derek McInnes and Scott Wilson, to name a few.

"You can't go on spending forever and, when guys like myself get a bit long in the tooth, the idea should be to have kids with a bit of experience ready to step in and take over."

Hendry himself was just a fresh-faced 18-year-old Highlander when he began his senior career at Dundee - surprisingly, as a striker.

The regular survival battles at Dens Park were a tough way for the young Hendry to serve his soccer apprenticeship, but he still believes the best way to learn is the hard way.

The player has since moved up from one bigger club to another, Dundee to pre-Kenny Dalglish Blackburn Rovers, on to Manchester City, returning to a very different Rovers backed by multi-millionaire Jack Walker, and now to Rangers.

These days, his role on the field may have changed, and he is certainly working in more glamorous surroundings than Dens - but he reckons it's all down to simple, honest, hard work.

> **"To be so involved in all the big prizes is certainly new for me, and it's a great feeling."**

Eyebrows were raised when Rangers paid £4 million for a man of his age, and on a four-year contract at that. But, for super-enthusiast Hendry, hunger and sweat can compensate for ageing limbs.

"I had to plug away at Dundee and gradually pick up things as I went along," explains the Keith-born defender, "so I know the value of hard work.

"When I was out injured for a couple of months last season, I had a very frustrating time, watching my club lose two consecutive matches for the first time - at a vital stage of the season - AND seeing Scotland lose a Euro 2000 qualifier to the Czech Republic.

"When I finally felt right, Dick Advocaat tried me in an Under-21 match first, and I was aware he was waiting to see how I went into my first tackle.

"So, when the referee had to take me aside and tell me to calm down, I think everyone knew that I was ready to return!

"The worst thing in the world for most players is being out and forced to watch from the sidelines. I'm a terrible spectator, so I was very glad to get back."

While the Czech defeat threatens to rob Colin of possibly his last international Finals appearance, he admits the Scottish Premier League losses were just as hard to bear.

The most patriotic member of Craig Brown's tartan squad, Colin has nevertheless played most of his club football outside his own country, so he admits to relishing every Rangers game. "Don't forget the club side of football is still a big adventure for me here," he explains. "The Scottish game is very different from when I was with Dundee, and I can only liken it to going to Old Trafford, Anfield or Highbury with Blackburn, when you seemed to produce a bit extra because of the big names you were playing against.

"You come up against that every week when you play for Rangers - only YOU'RE the big team there to be shot at - and it's not the easiest league in the world to work in at my age!

"However, Old Firm fans expect you to win everything, which wasn't always the case at my previous clubs, and I think the whole experience has added an edge to my game.

"It's very demanding, but maybe it's keeping me young! To be so involved in all the big prizes is certainly new for me, and it's a great feeling.

"Sure, if I'm not doing the things I'm supposed to, then fair enough, you can say I don't merit my place in the team. But I feel great, and there are a few years left in me yet." ■

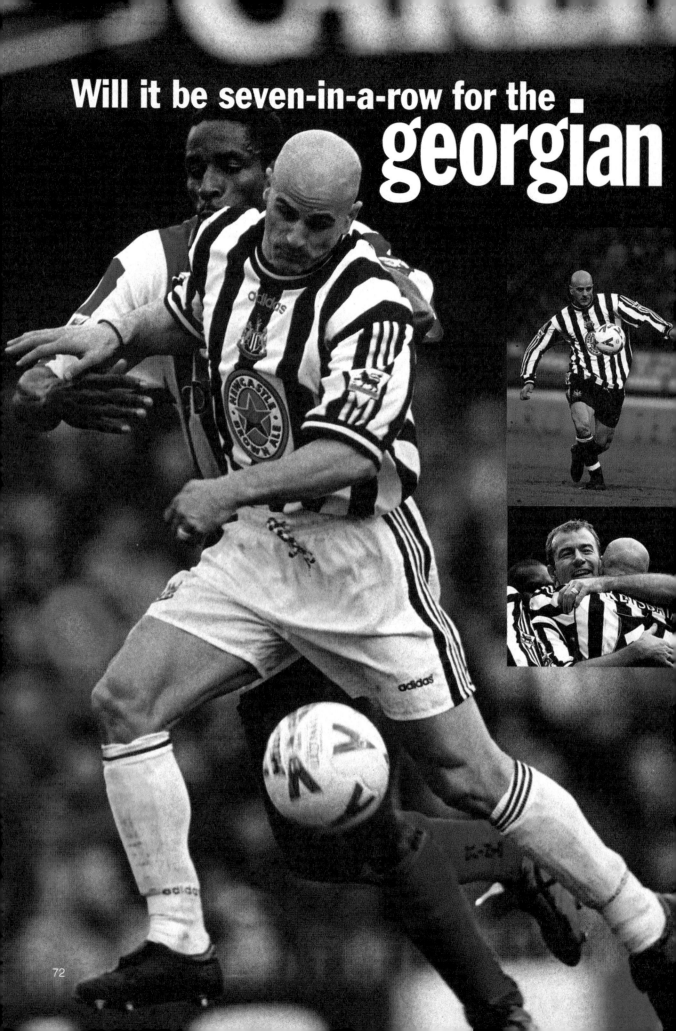

Will it be seven-in-a-row for the georgian

geordie?

rEMEMBER where you read it first. This season, Newcastle United will make it a hat-trick of consecutive FA Cup Final appearances.

All right, so The Topical Times does not possess a crystal ball and cannot be absolutely certain, but, with Temuri Ketsbaia on their books, the St James' Park outfit have to be in with a decent shout of making another trip to Wembley.

The Geordies' FA Cup Final defeat by Treble-winning Manchester United at the end of last season made it six Finals in a row for Ketsbaia. He had already appeared in two Greek Cup Finals for AEK Athens and in a couple of Georgian Finals for Dinamo Tbilisi before arriving in the North East.

It is a record of which the 31-year-old is rightly proud. He believes it proves that he is an important player.

To his dismay, Kenny Dalglish and Ruud Gullit, the two managers he has served under at Newcastle, haven't shared that view. He has been selected far too infrequently for his liking.

He believes his performances in a black and white shirt have warranted a permanent spot in the side. Just to add to his frustration, he reckons the

fans think along similar lines.

After months of scratching his head searching for a reason, he has finally come up with an answer, and not one he likes.

"I'm the kind of person that if I play for a team, I want to be an important player," he says. "It isn't enough for me just to be at a decent club.

"I don't want people to use me every now and again. I get angry when I play three games and then miss the next five before getting another chance. It shouldn't be like that.

"I think that every time I have played I have shown that I am a good player who shouldn't be discarded. I feel I should play in every game.

"I found it really strange to begin with but I'm beginning to understand it now. I also realise the situation will be hard to change.

"I can't escape the fact that I came from nowhere and nobody knew me before I arrived at St James' Park. That is the reason why I have struggled, and will continue to do so.

"It has made it hard for me because if I'm dropped, nobody cares too much, except myself. By comparison, if someone such as Arsenal's Dennis Bergkamp is left out, everyone wants to know why.

"I feel I have to score a hat-trick every time I go out in order to keep my place. I've found that very difficult and sometimes I get very frustrated and disappointed.

"I'm certain things would have been totally different if my name was Bergkamp instead of Ketsbaia. I feel I do almost as good a job as he does, yet I don't play anywhere near the number of games he does for Arsenal.

"I think that I have been a very important player for this club and have been involved in nearly all the good things that have happened in the last two years.

"I scored the goal that took the club into the lucrative Group stages of the Champions League a couple of years back. I also helped to turn games around during our runs to the

two Cup Finals.

"In fact, I ended last season as second-top scorer to Alan Shearer, and I played a lot fewer games than him.

"There shouldn't be a problem when you look at my record. I should play in every match."

Trying to reason with him that he is a crucial member of Gullit's squad is not to be recommended.

He goes on, "I don't want to listen when I hear people saying that Newcastle is a big club and every player is important. That is rubbish.

"I will never understand this squad system idea. It doesn't make any sense to me.

"Football is all about having your best players on the pitch. You can only have 11 best players, not 22.

"If one of your best players is injured or suspended, then you give someone a chance. You don't drop one of your best players for someone of less talent for no reason.

"It kills me when I play well in a game or score an important goal and then find out I'm dropped for the next one. I don't think it is right.

"If you play in one game, then miss three, how can you be at your best? It is no good for the players or the team. Everyone must know that the best players will play."

> **"I will never understand this squad system idea. It doesn't make any sense to me."**

Despite his evident concerns, he is delighted with life in the North East. He particularly enjoys the rapport he has with the fans.

He says, "They are always coming up to me in the street and in restaurants asking why I don't play more often. That just makes it even worse.

"They sing my name whether I play or not. Only Alan Shearer gets a bigger reception than me.

"It is not just because of my bald head. It is because I show that I'm doing the best I can for the club every time I play. They appreciate that.

"I just wish I had more chances to play in front of them. I know, though, that there is nothing I can do about that." ∎

better late than never!

Southampton's JAMES BEATTIE found his form just at the right time

JAMES BEATTIE found his scoring boots just in time to keep Southampton in the Premiership last season. The England Under-21 striker struggled to find the net for most of the campaign as the Saints battled against the growing threat of relegation. Things were looking bleak down at The Dell until Beattie suddenly found form reminiscent of his great hero Alan Shearer.

In the first nine months of the season, he'd managed only three League goals. But in the last two weeks of the season he changed all that in spectacular style.

First he scored with a spectacular volley to win the match against Leicester City. That took the Saints out of the bottom three at last.

The following week he scored the vital breakthrough goal at Wimbledon to put his team within touching distance of safety.

Then finally, on the nerve-wracking final day of the season, he made two brilliant assists for strike-partner Marian Pahars in a two-nil win over Everton. It was the end of a remarkable first season at The Dell for Beattie.

He'd played a huge part in keeping Southampton in the Premiership, just as Shearer had done seven years earlier.

Beattie had been a youth-team player at Blackburn Rovers when Shearer was scoring the goals that took Kenny Dalglish's team to a dramatic Premiership title in 1995, pipping Manchester United at the post. Although he was a big star, Shearer always had time for a word of advice for young James.

"Alan Shearer just had to be my hero at Blackburn," says James.

"All the young players at the club used to look up to him. Everything about him was worth watching, both on and off the pitch.

"Alan would make time for the younger lads. He'd always look out for me and ask how I'd got on at the weekend."

Of course, Shearer left Blackburn to join Newcastle but Beattie was never given the chance to replace him. Instead, he moved south to join Southampton, the club where Shearer first made his name.

It was to prove a very wise decision by Beattie. By the end of the season, Blackburn were relegated while Southampton saved themselves with that last day win over Everton.

"It was a bit strange to leave Blackburn. They are my home-town team and I'd been involved with them since I was very young," James goes on.

"They'd spotted me playing for my school team. At 17, I signed my first professional contract and thought I'd be there for years.

"It didn't quite work out that way. In the summer of 1998, Blackburn signed Kevin Davies from Southampton and I found myself moving in the opposite direction.

"At Blackburn, I still seemed to be a few years off playing Premiership football. When I joined Southampton, it was a very different story.

"It's always important to look at other players. I'm lucky to have had a close look at some of the best in the business.

"Coming down here gave me just the boost my career needed. I expected to play a few more games down here but it's worked out even better than that.

"Last season I was given a severe lesson in how to survive in the Premiership. From now on I'm far more interested in learning how to win things." ∎

"There were also two very special players to learn from at Southampton... Mark Hughes and Matt Le Tissier.

"I certainly picked up a few tricks from those two. Mark holds the ball up better than anybody in football and, of course, Matt is always capable of producing something out of the ordinary."

wim JONK Sheffield Wednesday

TOPICAL TIMES FOOTBALL BOOK

harry KEWELL Leeds Utd

quiz -time

1 Which foreign star won both the PFA and Football Writers' Footballer of the Year awards last season?

2 Which 'supersub' scored four goals after coming off the bench in a Premiership game last term?

3 Which Premiership player was sent off during Scotland's Euro 2000 clash with the Faroe Islands?

4 Which club plays its home games at Spotland?

5 Joe Royle guided which club to promotion last season?

6 Name the former Leeds United striker who helped Rangers to the Scottish "Treble" in 1998-99.

7 Which English club has won the League Championship most times?

8 Manchester United's Dwight Yorke was the joint top scorer in the Champions League last season. Which player tied with him?

9 Name the former England international who turned out for Hartlepool United last season.

10 True or False. Michael Owen's father used to play for Everton.

11 Which team did Arsenal agree to replay in last season's FA Cup Fifth Round despite winning the first game 2-1, and why?

12 Who managed England for just one game - against France - last year?

13 Which club created a new record last season by notching up 105 points?

14 Manchester United's Treble success last term was not unique in British football. Which team achieved it before Alex Ferguson's men?

15 Who became the first Peruvian to appear in an FA Cup Final?

16 Who won last season's UEFA Cup, and who did they beat in the Final?

17 Name the three Blackburn Rovers strikers who suffered relegation from the Premiership for the second successive time last year?

18 Who resigned as Wales coach after a 4-0 Euro 2000 qualifying defeat by Italy in June?

19 What is the nickname of Premiership new boys Watford?

20 With which club did Manchester United's Alex Ferguson begin his managerial career?

See question 15

answers

1. David Ginola (Spurs). **2.** Ole Gunnar Solskjaer for Manchester United, when they beat Nottingham Forest 8-1 in February, 1999. **3.** Matt Elliott (Leicester City). **4.** Rochdale. **5.** Manchester City. **6.** Rod Wallace. **7.** Liverpool (18 times). **8.** Andrei Shevchenko (Dynamo Kiev). **9.** Peter Beardsley. **10.** True-he made two appearances for the Toffees in the late 1960s. **11.** Sheffield United, because Marc Overmars' winning goal had been the result of unsporting conduct. **12.** Howard Wilkinson. **13.** Sunderland. **14.** Celtic, in 1967. **15.** Nolberto Solano. **16.** Parma. They beat Marseille 3-0. **17.** Nathan Blake, Ashley Ward and Matt Jansen. **18.** Bobby Gould. **19.** The Hornets. **20.** East Stirlingshire.

poacher turned goalkeeper!

The versatility of Sunderland's NIALL QUINN!

SUNDERLAND'S Niall Quinn has scored goals at every level, for club and country. But during a vital promotion battle away to Bradford City last season, he showed he could stop 'em as well as score 'em when he took over from regular goalkeeper Thomas Sorensen, who had gone off injured. Sunderland manager Peter Reid must have been pleased with his stand-in keeper...he kept a clean sheet in a 1-0 win! ■

record breakers!

The Topical Times talks to two men who just go on and on!

RECORD-BREAKING footballer Tony Ford has no desire to take it easy now that he has played more League games than any other outfield player in the history of the English game. Last season, Ford surpassed Terry Paine's record of 824 League games, 24 years after starting out as a 16-year-old with home-town club, Grimsby Town.

That feat was hardly the end for Tony, however. It merely set him up for the final leg in his greatest challenge.

With one record safely tucked away, the Mansfield Town defender is aiming to become a Millennium Man by notching up 1000 career games in the year 2000!

As he celebrated his 40th birthday at the end of last season, Tony was 30-odd games away from reaching his target.

Although age is rapidly catching up with him, the former Grimsby, Sunderland, Stoke, West Brom, Bradford and Scunthorpe man is determined to make one last entry into the record books.

He says, "Peter Shilton played over 1000 League games as a goalkeeper, but I think I will be hard pushed to get anywhere near that figure. It's probably an impossible target.

"I certainly think I can notch up 1000 career games, though. That would be a nice round figure. I am close enough to think about it but, at my age, it wouldn't be sensible to plan too far ahead.

"I will continue playing for as long as I can. This could be my last season, but I will only retire when I can't go on anymore.

"You are a long time retired. I have spoken to a lot of players who

Continued over page

825

Continued from previous page

have hung up their boots and the vast majority of them say that they packed up too soon."

The likes of Michael Owen, Wes Brown and Harry Kewell weren't even born when it all began for Tony back in 1975.

Derby County were the League Champions and West Ham the FA Cup holders. Fulham's Alan Mullery had just been crowned as Footballer of the Year.

The balance of power was certainly different in those days. Arsenal and Manchester United are the current footballing superpowers, but in 1975, the Gunners finished just four points above the relegation zone. As for United, they had just spent a season in the old Second Division!

Little of that mattered to Tony Ford, however. The 16-year-old was preparing to take the first steps in his professional career.

Tony recalls, "I made my debut in October, 1975. People have had to remind me that the opposition were Walsall. It was memorable in that it was my debut, but I can't really recall what happened.

"A few weeks later, I started my first game for Grimsby. I'm told that my first start coincided with Terry Paine breaking the League appearance record. I obviously never expected to break Terry's figure 24 years later!

"The fact that I have done so is

down to many factors. I have looked after myself and trained hard throughout my career, but I think I have been very lucky with injuries.

"Today, most kids will have suffered a bad injury before they end their apprenticeship. In 24 years, my worst injuries have been two hamstring problems that kept me out for five weeks each.

"My longevity is also down to positive thinking. Once you reach 30, people begin to suggest that you are ready to retire. If you believe that, you are bound to feel old. I never accepted that.

"Many players in their mid-30's are still going strong. There are some who are still playing at the highest level like Everton's Dave Watson.

"I have been sensible during my career and that is also important. Today, many clubs tell players what and when to eat, and when to sleep. I have never been that scientific, but I've always looked after myself.

> **"It was memorable in that it was my debut, but I can't really recall what happened."**

"Gordon Strachan apparently prolonged his career by taking seaweed tablets. I haven't done that, but I do take vitamin pills to help me along.

"You have to be single-minded and listen to your body before you listen to the 'experts.' If I have been called a veteran, I have always ignored it.

"It was nice to eventually break Terry Paine's record, however. As a kid, I used to collect sticker books and he was a big name when I was growing up. He wasn't my hero, though. That was Jimmy Greaves.

"When I went past Terry's figure of 824 games, Mansfield invited him to the game. He is living in South Africa now and couldn't make it, but he sent his best wishes and urged me to beat him by a good distance."

When Tony finally calls it a day, he will have special memories to recall for both club and country.

He adds, "Club-wise, the best moment was helping Grimsby to successive promotions from the old Fourth Division to the old Second Division in 1979 and 1980.

"After being in the lower leagues for such a long time, it was great for Blundell Park to host games against big clubs like Chelsea and Leeds, who had dropped into the old Second Division.

"We were the toast of the town for a while and it meant a lot to me as a local lad.

"Personally, I can't beat playing for England B in 1989. I was part of the squad that went to Scandinavia and Switzerland and I played in a couple of games.

"I was at West Brom at the time, but I was called into the squad along with a few young hopefuls like Paul Gascoigne, David Platt and Steve Bull.

"England manager, Bobby Robson, wanted to see how they would do at international level. If I was there just to complement them and make up the numbers, I don't mind.

"It was an honour just to be selected in the first place. A year later, Gazza, Platt and Bully were at the World Cup in Italy. Unknowns one minute, national heroes the next!" ∎

864

tHERE was one man who beat Tony to the magical 1000 appearance mark... Stenhousemuir player/manager Graeme Armstrong. He broke the Scottish record for appearances last December in a game for the Warriors against East Stirlingshire, his 864th senior League appearance.

His 1000th senior appearance couldn't have been better timed...a Scottish Cup-tie v. Rangers at Ibrox Park in last January, before 50,000 fans. As a gesture to his fantastic achievement, the Glasgow giants presented Graeme with a crystal decanter before the match. Unfortunately, Greame couldn't celebrate a giant-killing victory to mark the occasion...Stenhousemuir went down two-nil!

Like Tony, Graeme cannot remember his first game all those years ago, but he doesn't have to be reminded who the opposition were.

"It was a trial for Meadowbank against Stirling Albion, but I ended signing for Albion. Funnily enough, I went to Meadowbank later on and spent the bulk of my career there. "

Not content with one record, Graeme broke another in May 1999 when he became the first manager to steer 'Muir to promotion, after only five months in charge. ∎

king kev

KEVIN PHILLIPS is Top Of The Pops

KEVIN PHILLIPS was told he would be treated like a god if he made a name for himself with Sunderland. The highly-rated striker dreamed about the prospect when he arrived at The Stadium of Light in the summer of 1997 following a bargain £325,000 switch from Watford.

Deep down, however, Phillips didn't even expect to be a regular in manager Peter Reid's team.

Despite receiving high praise from his new manager, Kevin believed he would spend his first season on Wearside playing second fiddle to a big-name hitman.

The last thing he expected to do was enter Sunderland's record books but, by the end of his first campaign at the club, he had done just that!

Now, after helping Sunderland into the Premiership last season, Phillips is worshipped by the red-and-white hordes just as he was told he would be.

Not bad for a player who feared for his career just a couple of years ago.

Kevin explains, "Glenn Roeder spotted me playing for non-league Baldock Town when he was Watford manager.

"Glenn had a lengthy spell with Newcastle United in the 1980's and he told me that the North East was a special area in which to play football. Everything he told me has been spot on.

"My time at the club has been amazing. I arrived at Sunderland as something of an unknown, but I had an incredible first season, scoring loads of goals and breaking a few records along the way.

"Brian Clough held the club record of scoring in six consecutive games, but I managed seven. I also ended up becoming the first Sunderland player to score 30 goals in one season since Brian did so in 1963.

"I will never forget that season, but I was devastated when all our efforts resulted in nothing. Despite my goals, we missed out on promotion after losing to Charlton in the Play-Off Final. That took the shine off the season.

"Thankfully, we made up for that disappointment by winning the First

in

at Sunderland's Stadium of Light

> **"The North East is a special area in which to play football".**

Division championship last term. I missed a large chunk of the season through injury, but I could handle that because we ended up being promoted to the Premiership.

"When I arrived at the club, Peter Reid told me that I was the man who would score the goals that would take Sunderland up.

"I didn't really believe him. I thought he was just saying that to keep me happy! It was a boost to my confidence, but I still expected a £4 million striker to arrive. I was amazed when it didn't happen.

"Nobody knew who I was in Sunderland, but I knew I would have to live with that anonymity until I started scoring goals."

Once Kevin started, the goals didn't stop. He hit 35 in all during

his first season at the club, enough to earn an England "B" call-up.

Despite missing almost half of last season, Kevin still managed to break double figures as Sunderland walked away with the First Division championship.

He also won his first England cap in the friendly against Hungary last May.

But it could all have been so different had he failed to beat a career-threatening injury during his time at Watford.

Kevin recalls, "I damaged the ligament underneath the arch in my right foot while playing for Watford at Reading. There was a hole in the ligament and it completely baffled everybody at the club.

"Neither the physio nor club surgeon at Watford had ever seen an injury like it before. It was certainly career-threatening because nobody had a clue how to cure the problem.

"Initially, the foot was put in a cast for two weeks, but it didn't heal properly.

"If it had been immobilised for six weeks it might have healed, but we didn't know that at the time.

"It took six months before it was properly diagnosed. I actually owe my career to Bob McKenny, the club surgeon at Watford, because he resolved the problem and put me back on track.

"I was very worried about my future before Bob sorted everything out. I had gone to Vicarage Road from part-time football and knew all about life outside the game.

"I worked at Dixons stacking televisions and also drove a van, delivering radiators. After tasting life as a professional footballer, I didn't want to go back to be being a van driver.

"I appreciate what I have and that's why I aim to make the most of my career and achieve everything I possibly can." ∎

a century of soccer
no5. 1970-79

Player of the decade: Kevin Keegan

KEVIN KEEGAN was the ultimate example to every kid who has the determination to make the most of what ability they have and carve out a career in football. Though not blessed with an abundance of natural talent, Keegan worked ceaselessly on his game and rose from being a scrawny kid from Doncaster to become the captain of England.

Throughout his career, both as a player and subsequently as manager, he never ceased to amaze observers with his unending supply of energy and enthusiasm for the game. Both on and off the pitch, he simply left others in his wake.

Spotted by Liverpool manager Bill Shankly while playing for Scunthorpe United, he signed for Liverpool in 1971 and became a legend on Merseyside.

During six memorable years with the club, he won the European Cup, three League Championships, two UEFA Cups and the FA Cup.

His most successful on-field partnership was as a twin striker alongside John Toshack. With 5ft 8in Keegan dwarfed alongside the giant Welshman, they were known as the Little and Large of football, with an uncanny and instinctive goalscoring partnership.

Keegan's Liverpool career ended triumphantly as they beat Borussia Moenchengladbach to win the 1977 European Cup. He narrowly missed out on a treble, having clinched the League title but losing to Manchester United in the FA Cup Final.

Keegan's one FA Cup winner's medal had been collected after his two goals helped to chalk up a 3-0 Wembley win over Newcastle United in 1974. Ironically, that was the club to which he would later become a Messiah twice - as the influential player who led them to promotion in 1984, then as one of the club's most popular managers a decade later.

He won 63 caps for England, and was appointed manager of his country last season. ■

Milestones:

1971 Arsenal match the feat of their North London rivals, Spurs, when they become the second club this century to win the League and FA Cup Double.

1974 League football is played on a Sunday for the first time.

1976 Goal average is scrapped by the Football League and replaced by goal difference.

1978 The transfer tribunal system is introduced, whereby a Football League panel sets a fee when the two clubs cannot agree on a player's valuation.

1979 The first all-British £1 million transfer fee is set as Trevor Francis moves from Birmingham City to Nottingham Forest.

Other prominent players of the 1970s

PAT JENNINGS. Northern Ireland goalkeeper who became the fourth British footballer to appear in more than 100 internationals. Won 119 caps, which was a record at the time. Won the FA Cup, two League Cups and the UEFA Cup with Spurs. FA Cup winner with Arsenal in 1979. Only goalkeeper to play for both Spurs and Arsenal.

BILLY BREMNER. Tough and dynamic Scot, who captained Don Revie's Leeds United side, which won all before them. Picked up 54 caps for Scotland.

EMLYN HUGHES. Team-mate of Keegan. Known as "Crazy Horse", Hughes captained Liverpool to 4 Championships,1 FA Cup, 2 European Cups and 1 UEFA Cup. He also won a League Cup medal with Wolves. 62 England caps.

a fox's tale!

Leicester's STEVE GUPPY tells all!

S TEVE GUPPY has every reason to feel confident. An established Premiership performer, he possesses the kind of left foot that most can only dream about.

Yet the Leicester City wing-back is a bag of nerves in the dressing room before a match. Try as he might, he just can't sit still.

Indeed, he gets so tense and edgy that his team mates have nicknamed him Nervous Norris!

Guppy's apprehension doesn't stem from a lack of belief in his ability, however. It is just that he is so desperate to make the most of his talents every time he steps onto a pitch.

The 30-year-old took a late and unconventional route into professional football and doesn't want to let life in the Premiership pass him by. Every one of his pin-point crosses is vital.

He may walk around the Foxes' training ground most of the time wearing the yellow bib awarded to the worst trainer of the week - it even has the words "I've had a Guppy" written across it - but when it comes to matchdays, he makes sure he is fully tuned in.

It is this attitude which has made him a favourite of manager Martin O'Neill. He believes Guppy is the best left-footed player in the country.

Although known for a tendency to exaggerate, the Irishman was able to point to a telling statistic last season to back up his assessment. For most of that time Guppy headed the list of leading cross-makers in the Premiership.

Leicester's second appearance in three years at Wembley last March to contest the Worthington Cup Final was down in no short measure to Guppy's wing wizardry.

It is all a far cry from the time he had to be bullied by a friend to take up the game he had turned his back

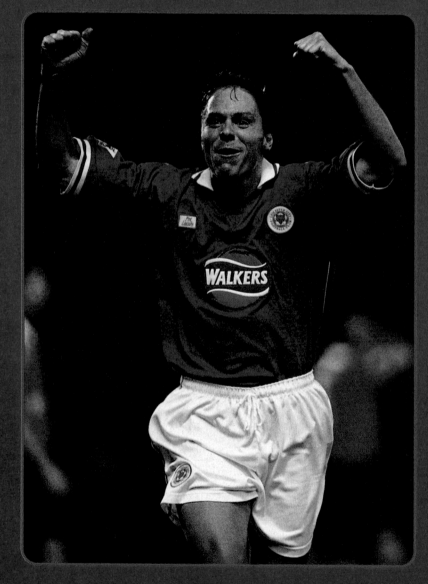

on as a teenager.

"I gave up football for two years from the age of 16," says Steve. "I had received so many knockbacks in my attempts to get a League club that I decided I'd had enough.

"I just lost interest. I'd had trials and heard rumours of clubs being interested but nothing seemed to be

happening. I was sick of putting myself under so much pressure only to be rejected.

"To be honest, I didn't really miss it and it was only when a mate kept on at me to join his Sunday team in Southampton a couple of years later that I gave it another go. It wasn't long before my appetite for

the game returned and I was playing three matches every weekend.

"It was then I started practising on my own and began to think I could still make it as a professional footballer."

Joining then non-league Wycombe Wanderers a couple of years later proved to be the perfect stepping stone.

He goes on, "I joined them when I was 20 and had five great years there - four in the Football Conference, followed by a season in the League after winning promotion.

"As a semi-professional I had to find a job. Fortunately, the Chairman, Mr Beeks, owned a construction company and took me on as a labourer.

"I wasn't particularly brilliant at it and, in all honesty, I didn't do much work. It was a bit of a dead end job. My heart wasn't really in it.

"Really, I was a full-time, part-time footballer because whenever I had the chance, I'd seek out the nearest playing field to the site on which we were working and practise for as long as possible. My boss didn't really mind.

"Looking back, I should have done something better with that time. I really should have gone to college to study something."

Any regrets soon melted away when Kevin Keegan bought him for his emerging Newcastle United side. It appeared to be a dream move, yet it wasn't long before the feelings he had as a teenager resurfaced.

He says, "I was only at St James' Park for three months, so I didn't really get to show what I could do.

"I probably joined at the wrong time because the club was bombing along, and I wasn't involved in any way.

"All I did was sit in the stands watching. That was all right for a while because I learned a few things but I soon became desperate. I just wasn't getting a game. It took me back a bit to when I was 16.

"I felt I was good enough to play in the Premiership but it was pretty clear that I would have to get away from St James' Park if I was going to prove it.

"Fortunately, John Rudge signed me for Port Vale and it was there things really began to take off. It was a step back to go forward again. I actually started quite slowly at Vale Park and it took me a long while to settle in. The facilities at Vale didn't bear comparison to those at Wycombe, never mind Newcastle, but Rudge and his coach, Billy Dearden, taught me a heck of a lot about playing League football. Without them I wouldn't be where I am today."

After a couple of seasons in the Potteries, Martin O'Neill, who had been his manager at Wycombe, swooped to take him to Leicester.

"I'm indebted to Martin," says Steve. "Aside from my Dad, he has been the biggest influence on my career.

"He took a chance on bringing me into the Premiership when it looked as though nobody else was interested. I'll always be grateful to him for that.

"Martin hasn't changed one bit. He has always jumped around on the sidelines when watching games.

"He was just as passionate and involved when Wycombe were playing teams like Kettering as he is now when we visit places like Liverpool, Manchester United and Arsenal. The only difference is that the media have picked up on it because he is on a bigger stage." ■

> "I'm indebted to Martin. Aside from my Dad, he has been the biggest influence on my career."

KARLHEINZ RIEDLE is happy to take a back seat to messrs OWEN and FOWLER!

supporting

KARLHEINZ RIEDLE'S role at Liverpool as understudy to both Michael Owen and Robbie Fowler is a job that most strikers would dread.

Owen is arguably the hottest property in world football following his exploits in the 1998 World Cup. His sensational goal against Argentina transformed him from boy wonder into a world-famous superstar.

Then you have Fowler, the Liverpool-born scoring machine, who has already broken Anfield records previously held by club legends Roger Hunt and Ian Rush.

Few strikers could ever hope to break up such a deadly double act and Riedle knows it is a massive task.

Not many challenges have been beyond Riedle during his outstanding career. Few footballers can say they have won both the World Cup and European Champions League, as Karlheinz has done with Germany and Borussia Dortmund.

However, with a glorious career to look back on, Riedle is happy to take a back seat at Anfield.

Karlheinz explains, "Michael and Robbie are both world-class strikers. When I came to Liverpool from Dortmund in the summer of 1997, I did not expect to find such good players in the forward positions.

"I was immediately impressed by Robbie, but I was very surprised by Michael's performances in my first year at the club. Then again, I wasn't the only one to be taken aback by his talent!

"It's not easy when you have two lads like them competing with you. I have played at the top level for many years now, but there is nothing that I can teach Michael or Robbie because they are both so talented.

"I have played in World Cups and European finals, but despite my experience, I really don't believe there is anything I can show them to make them better players."

Two years into his Liverpool career, Riedle can look back on as many substitute appearances as starts for the Merseysiders.

His value to the club was underlined late last season, however, when both Fowler and Owen were absent for long periods. Owen's hamstring injury and Fowler's six-match suspension meant that Riedle was the only established striker available to manager Gerard Houllier.

The return of the deadly duo earlier this season signalled a return to the bench, but Riedle is content with his trouble-shooting role.

"People ask if I find it difficult when I am forced to sit and watch from the bench, but it is not a problem for me," admits the former Lazio striker.

"I don't become frustrated when the manager decides to rest me. It's only natural for him to do that and play Robbie and Michael instead.

"I know I am fit enough to score goals and I feel as though I can continue to do so until I am 36 or 37. Resting

> "There is nothing that I can teach Michael or Robbie because they are both so talented."

role

me from time to time is the right thing to do because it keeps me fresh.

"Michael and Robbie are Liverpool's future. I am in my mid-30s, so you can see why they are the favoured partnership at the club.

"I am happy for them and have no reason to be jealous. I have had my titles and cups and there is little that I have not achieved in the game.

"It is obviously better when you play all the time, and I don't mean to suggest that I am happy to take it easy by playing every now and then. We all want to play, but I can see the reasons why I am used less often than I would like.

"I am experienced enough to know that every big club needs more good players than it can fit into the team. There are players like me at Manchester United, Arsenal and Chelsea who also have to deal with not playing every week.

"The idea of a big squad is to help you compete for trophies. We haven't done that in my time at Liverpool, but I would really like to end my career having helped the club bring some silverware back to Anfield."∎

Steve Simonsen

youth

Give young keepers a chance, says Leeds United's NIGEL MARTYN

IGEL MARTYN and David Seaman demonstrated the best of British goalkeeping last season in a 90-minute master-class at Elland Road, when Leeds United played Arsenal.

Some superb saves by Martyn helped Leeds win 1-0, to end Arsenal's, and Seaman's, hopes of retaining the Premiership title.

But Seaman was even more impressive at the other end. The Arsenal man did enough to keep ahead of his friend and rival, and remain as England's number one keeper.

Now Martyn goes into the new millennium hoping this is the year that he can find something extra, to enable him finally to take over the international spot from the Arsenal star. The confidence he gained from helping Leeds qualify for the UEFA Cup, and emerge as serious challengers to Manchester United, Arsenal and Chelsea, will help Martyn press his claims for the England place.

Last year he was content just to be in the shadow of Seaman.

"For me, Dave is still very much the top dog. The rest of us are just battling to be his back-up man," said Martyn.

"He is so cool, makes very few mistakes, and has seen and done everything in the game. He is the

policy

total package.

"I've no doubts Dave will be around for a good while yet. I've heard that he wants to carry on until the 2002 World Cup, and it wouldn't surprise me if he achieves that.

"Forty is the magic age for goalkeepers now. Ever since Peter Shilton extended his career beyond that figure, we are all striving to do the same.

"If Dave manages that, I'll be in for a long wait. I just hope I'll be around when a replacement is being discussed.

"But I won't worry, because there's nothing I can do about it. I can only concentrate on my own form.

"As a goalkeeper, you can't afford to look too far ahead. You're only one blunder away from losing your hard-earned reputation.

"You are only as good as your last game. You don't get many opportunities at international level.

"There is always a lot of pressure playing for England. If you make a mistake, there is not much to fall back on.

"Although you are under

> ## " The lack of young up-and-coming goalkeepers in the Premiership is a big worry. There are not many breaking through. "

pressure at club level, it's not quite the same. You know that one error is not going to cost you your career."

For the time being, Seaman (36) and Martyn (33) look secure from serious challenge by younger keepers, although Spurs' Ian Walker is now back to his best form.

Further back, Richard Wright (Ipswich) and Steve Simonsen (Everton) are the most promising of the next generation, but lack experience at top level. Too many foreign goalkeepers are hindering

> ## " The foreign invasion is already having an impact. "

the progress of young goalkeepers in England.

Seaman and Martyn came into the game when competition from foreigners was not a problem.

"The lack of young up-and-coming goalkeepers in the Premiership is a big worry. There are not many breaking through," says Nigel.

"We could be storing up problems for the future. The foreign invasion is already having an impact.

"There are some good young keepers in the lower divisions, but Premiership clubs don't want to take a chance on them like they used to.

"The stakes are too high. Everybody wants a proven international goalkeeper.

"In the old days, the lower leagues were the breeding ground for future England keepers. I started at Bristol Rovers, David Seaman got his early experience at Peterborough, and Tim Flowers learned the business at Wolves.

"Going further back, Ray Clemence began at Scunthorpe and Gordon Banks at Chesterfield.

"I'm just glad I came through when I did. If I was starting now, I'd be in the same position as a lot of young keepers in the lower divisions.

"The trickle through to the top has dried up. Top clubs automatically look abroad, and you can understand it because foreign players are generally a cheaper option.

"At the moment the standard of goalkeeping in this country is still good. But there could be a problem in a few years' time, unless more youngsters are given a chance in the Premiership."

As it is, the situation is likely to help Martyn retain his place in the England squad. He has been outstanding in the last year behind a young and talented Leeds team.

"George Graham made us into a very well organised unit, and David O'Leary has taken things on from there," he says. "It's the best defence I've played behind.

"For a goalkeeper, the toughest thing is to maintain concentration when you are not having a lot to do. But I'm not complaining.

"I'll be very happy if I don't have anything to do this season." ■

bantam wait!

Success at long last for Bradford City's GARY WALSH!

GARY WALSH made his full debut for Manchester United during the 1986-87 season, but injuries, illness and sheer bad luck have had such an effect on his career that he had to wait until last season to enjoy his first campaign as an ever-present.

What a season it was, though. The Bradford City goalkeeper played a major part in helping The Bantams win promotion to the Premiership and secure their return to the top flight for the first time since 1927.

Finally, Walsh enjoyed some long overdue glory. Despite spending 11 years at Old Trafford, Gary always missed out on the silverware. A move to Middlesbrough in 1995 promised much, but turned sour when he played no part in the club's two trips to Wembley in 1997.

If Walsh's career had followed the path many believed it would, the 31-year-old could have been challenging the likes of David Seaman and Nigel Martyn for the England goalkeeping jersey.

You don't make your debut as an 18-year-old at Manchester United unless you have the ability to go right to the top. Just look at the likes of Ryan Giggs, David Beckham and Paul Scholes.

Unlike that star trio, however, Gary's career has been blighted by injuries. To make matters worse, most of his problems have baffled the doctors and kept him out of the game for months.

Gary explains, "A few years ago, I had to move my bed downstairs into the lounge at my parents' home because I had a full length plaster on my leg for nine months and couldn't climb.

"My mum and dad worked during the day, so rather than spend the whole time sitting around on my own, I would go to bed at 8.30 in the morning when they left for work and sleep until they came home about five.

"I had their company and that of my girlfriend until late evening. Then I'd stay up all night and watch films on satellite TV!"

The injury was nothing as simple as a broken leg, however. The foot injury sustained in training wrote a new chapter in the medical records!

"I broke a bone called the talus bone," Gary recalls. "It was the first break of its kind recorded anywhere in the world.

"The specialists didn't know what to do and I had two unsuccessful operations. The money United spent on my treatment must have been astronomical.

"Eventually, I had a third op. The idea was to take a piece of bone from my hip and graft it on to my foot. If it didn't work, I would have been finished as a footballer.

"Fortunately, the operation was a success and I was playing again within eight months."

That setback was the third major blow in his young career. A severe kick on the head, followed by a mystery virus, kept Gary on the sidelines.

"I was playing for United in a tour game in Bermuda when I went down at the feet of one of their forwards," he recalls. "He came in with a bad challenge and the next thing I knew about was waking up in hospital the next day.

"The guy who did it suffered as well. He kicked me so hard that he damaged his knee and had to go in a wheelchair for a few days!

"I was out for three months with my head injury. I then developed the virus which cost me another seven months. Whenever a flu bug went around the dressing room, I would always catch it first!"

Once Gary had overcome his ailments, an even bigger worry arrived on the scene at Old Trafford — Peter Schmeichel! After valiantly battling with the Great Dane for the number one shirt, Gary eventually gave up and opted to move to Middlesbrough.

"I should have left United sooner than I did and I now regret not doing so. I had to leave, even though manager Alex Ferguson wanted me to stay.

"I wanted first-team football and Alex was very understanding. I wasn't guaranteed to play at Middlesbrough by any means, but at least I didn't have Peter Schmeichel blocking my way.

"Most people say that you can only step down when you leave United, but I must be the exception. I went from playing in front of 500 people for the reserves to full houses at The Riverside every week.

"That's why I never regret leaving Old Trafford. The move to Middlesbrough didn't work out as I would have liked, but at least I was playing more often.

"Moving to Bradford two years ago did me no harm, however. I was only 29 at the time, but because I have been around for so long, people think I am older than I am. They think I am a veteran!

"I saw my move to Valley Parade as my graduation as a goalkeeper. I served a ten-year apprenticeship at United and Middlesbrough and arrived at Bradford as a fully-qualified 'keeper.

"I was in a rut at Middlesbrough. Chris Kamara, then manager of Bradford, rescued me and put his faith in me. I was desperate for an opportunity and last season's promotion was a fantastic achievement for everybody at the club." ∎

> "It was the first break of its kind recorded anywhere in the world."

mikael FORSSELL Chelsea

TOPICAL TIMES FOOTBALL BOOK

escape route!

... for Coventry City's

MUHAMMED KONJIC

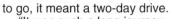

tHE next time a Premiership footballer moans about the number of games he has to play or grumbles about being stressed out, he should be sent for a little chat with Coventry City's centre-back, Muhammed Konjic.

A couple of minutes in the Bosnian's company might just convince him of how lucky he is to be paid more in a week than most people earn in a year just for playing football.

The £2 million signing from Monaco knows what real pressure is all about.

Not so long ago, football was the last thing on his mind. He was just doing his best to keep himself and his family alive as civil war raged in the former Yugoslavia.

His troubles weren't over even when he eventually managed to escape the fighting. There was still a near-fatal car crash to overcome before he could safely resume his playing career.

He says, "I was in Bosnia in the war for one-and-a-half years. I did whatever I could to take care of myself and my family.

"I didn't have a choice. The Serbian and Croatian armies invaded my country and attacked my village. When that happens, you only have two choices - to fight or to die.

"In six months, 300,000 of my countrymen and women died. We lost 500,000 in four years.

"We sent our women and children away from home as refugees to escape the fighting. It meant I was there, in my house with my father and brothers, with the bombs coming down.

"Everywhere around me was bombed and broken, but I was always an optimist and always tried to believe I would get away.

"Yet we had no food, no water, no medical equipment or medicines, no electricity. Nothing. All we had was hope."

In the end, his football ability provided a route to safety, although the deal which took him from FC Sarajevo to NK Zagreb in Croatia was unusual to say the least.

He goes on, "I was sold for food. There was no point in paying cash because money did not mean anything. The blockades meant the food could not get in and you might need £200 for a few loaves of bread."

Yet, the trauma didn't end there. He was almost killed on the journey to his new life in a different country.

"There were still so many army roadblocks and we feared for what might happen," he says. "So we tried to find routes to avoid them.

"I was in Tuzla trying to get to Osic. It should take 90 minutes but, because of the way we had to go, it meant a two-day drive.

"It was such a long journey that my driver fell asleep. We smashed into a bus and were sent down a ditch. The car fell 20 metres and turned three somersaults. I smashed the bones in both my arms on the dashboard.

"My arms were in plaster but I still had to play football. They paid me only £100 per month but, more importantly, they gave me food, which I could send back to my parents in parcels every two months."

It wasn't long before his talents were recognised across Europe and, after a stint in French football, he signed for Gordon Strachan's team halfway through last season.

He ends, "I always watched English football and loved it. My people still don't understand how it is possible to work that hard every match, to fight for every tackle."

Although he only appeared in three matches for the Sky Blues last season, Konjic is determined to establish himself in the side and play against the Premiership's world-class strikers. ■

aerial warfare!

Aston Villa and Sheffield Wednesday

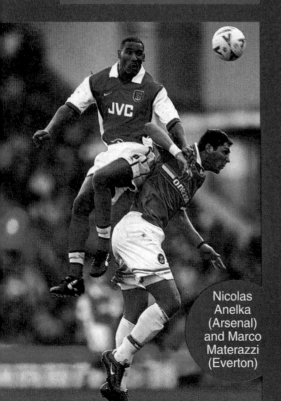

Alan Shearer (Newcastle United) and Stephen Carr (Spurs)

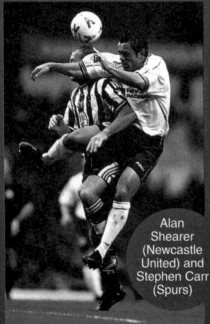

Nicolas Anelka (Arsenal) and Marco Materazzi (Everton)

Jaap Stam (Manchester United) and Carsten Jancker (Bayern Munich)

Muzzy Izzet (Leicester City) and Robbie Earle and Andy Roberts (Wimbledon)

Duncan Ferguson (Newcastle) and Jamie Garracher (Liverpool)

Gustavo Poyet (Chelsea) and Mark Kennedy (Wimbledon)

Chris Perry (Wimbledon) and Tore Andre Flo (Chelsea)

ALLUM DAVIDSON had to endure a relegation battle with Blackburn Rovers last season, but it could have been far worse for the Scottish defender. Just three years ago, Davidson turned his back on football after becoming totally disillusioned with the game. Had he stuck to his guns and walked away for good, he would probably now be spending his days sat behind a desk in an office, wondering about what might have been.

The 23-year-old found himself going through the motions at Scottish Premier Division side, St Johnstone. Fearful of wasting his time pursuing a pointless career, Callum decided to stop playing and concentrate on his studies instead.

"Playing in the Premiership and then breaking into the Scotland squad certainly backs up my decision to return to the game."

Fortunately for the Stirling-born player, he was persuaded to return to the game. It was the best advice he has ever received.

Three years on, Davidson is a £1.75 million member of Brian Kidd's first-team and a regular in the Scotland squad.

Callum is quick to acknowledge that his sabbatical from the game brought about his lucky break.

He admits, "My current situation for both club and country is fantastic. Playing in the Premiership and then breaking into the Scotland squad certainly backs up my decision to return to the game.

"While I was playing as a part-timer with St Johnstone, I had decided to give up football. I was studying Civil Engineering at university at the same time and eventually, I had to choose between the two.

"The simple fact of the matter was that I wasn't enjoying my football. I had fallen out of love with the game. I wasn't playing well for Saints and whenever I played, I was used as a left winger or a central midfielder.

"It just wasn't working out for

second choice!

me. The fact that I was only playing on a part-time basis meant I wasn't fit enough to come up to scratch.

"Being at university all the time, I found it too hard to combine both studying and playing.

"The football wasn't going too well and the manager at the time, Paul Sturrock, told me that he was going to release me if I didn't become a full-time player.

"Considering I was halfway through a four-year course, I decided to quit the football.

"Although I wasn't playing for St Johnstone, I continued to keep myself fit by training with lower league club, Livingston. I wasn't too concerned about getting back into the game but I wanted to maintain

"My luck changed as soon as I went back to McDiarmid Park".

my fitness just in case.

After a while, though, I really began to miss playing. I wanted to get back.

"I am indebted to John Blackley, the assistant manager of St Johnstone at the time, because he persisted with me and eventually persuaded me to go back to the club and give it another go.

"I decided to return to football on a full-time basis, so I had to opt out of the Civil Engineering course. It is something I can go back to in the future, but it all depends on how well the football goes from now on.

"I have had quite a lucky turnaround. It was good to be taken back by St Johnstone in the first place, but to then find myself earning a move to Blackburn has been fantastic. I know I have been fortunate and I count my lucky stars!

"My luck changed as soon as I went back to McDiarmid Park. After being used in several positions previously, I was put in at left-back and that is where I have been ever since.

"It was a big decision to quit the game when I did, but at the time it was the easiest choice I have ever had to make because I hated the game. It was as simple as that.

"Now, I am loving every minute. Playing for Blackburn and Scotland is a totally different scale to what I expected."

Although Callum is now first-choice left back at Ewood Park, he admits that he almost sank without trace in his first few weeks at the club.

He goes on, "My first three months at Blackburn were a complete nightmare. I pulled my hamstring virtually as soon as I arrived and it was a bad pull that took ages to shake off.

"Once I overcame that, I made my debut in a 4-1 home defeat by Arsenal. The result was bad enough, but I picked up another injury and didn't play again that season.

"It made my early days at Blackburn very hard. I found it difficult to get to know anybody because, instead of showing my worth on the training pitch, I was lying on the treatment table all day.

"I wasn't involved at all and it would have been very easy to become disillusioned and fall away. I was just lucky enough to be able to get a few training sessions in at the end of the season.

"My early problems are all behind me now and the move has been terrific. International recognition was talked about when I was in Scotland, but it's only since I came down to England that I have broken through. It has been a magic move for me" ■

the man responsible for Callum's return to football, John Blackley, first saw Callum playing for Dundee F.C. Youths as a thirteen-year-old and at once saw the potential the young defender possessed.

"Callum's attitude even in these early days was spot-on. He had a desire to win and an eagerness to work hard. I'm sure it was that attitude that got him through those nightmare opening months at Ewood Park.

"He can be accused of being aggressive, but that aggression comes with bravery in the tackle and wholehearted competitiveness."

John, now assistant manager at Dundee United, has worked with some of the

best left-backs in Scotland and at the moment rates United's Maurice Malpas as the best.

However, he reckons Callum can be as good or even better. That was why he had no hesitation in persuading Callum to return to football

"Callum has the chance...and the ability...to become one of Scotland's best-ever left-backs, and, barring injury, has a long and satisfying Scotland career ahead of him," declares John.

michael **OWEN** Liverpool

TOPICAL TIMES FOOTBALL BOOK

darren **HUCKERBY** Coventry City

TOPICAL TIMES FOOTBALL BOOK

DOLISED at Anfield as the King of the Kop, Kenny Dalglish achieved more success on both sides of the border than any other player. By the time he signed for Liverpool in 1977, he had already won four Scottish Championships, two Scottish Cups and a Scottish League Cup.

The move to Liverpool was seen as something of a sterner test, especially as he was bought to replace another legend - Kevin Keegan. Would he measure up?

The answer was rapped out emphatically over the next ten years as he became one of the most revered players ever to grace the Anfield turf.

A scorer of great goals, he was also the guiding light for a succession of players around him who would develop into Liverpool greats themselves.

In particular, Ian Rush, who would become the club's all-time top goalscorer, was shaped and guided by the influence of Dalglish alongside him.

Glasgow-born, Dalglish wrote his own way into the record-books. He was the first player to score more than 100 goals in both Scotland and England, won a record 102 Scottish international caps and equalled Denis Law's total of 30 goals for Scotland.

Along the way, he collected three European Cups, five League Championships, four League Cups and two Footballer of the Year awards.

Immediately after the Heysel Stadium disaster in 1985, he was appointed player-manager of Liverpool, and guided his side to the League and FA Cup Double the following season, adding a further two titles and an FA Cup win before resigning in 1991.

His importance to Merseyside had also been demonstrated in the wake of the Hillsborough disaster which claimed the lives of 96 Liverpool fans, as his firm but compassionate leadership helped the community in its grief.

Following a seven-month break from football, Dalglish returned as manager of Blackburn Rovers and guided the club to the Championship in 1995. He then took over as manager of Newcastle United, taking them to the 1998 FA Cup Final.

In June 1999, he returned to Celtic as Director of Football.

Milestones:

1981. Liverpool are the first British club to win the European Cup three times. They are to win it a fourth time in 1984.

1981. Football League introduces three points for a win.

1981. The League's first artificial pitch is installed by Queens Park Rangers.

1984. The Home International Championships are disbanded. Northern Ireland win the final competition.

1984. Stirling Albion beat Selkirk 20-0 in the Scottish Cup to record Britain's biggest score of the century.

1985. Football witnesses two disasters as 56 spectators are killed in the Bradford fire and 39 die at the European Cup Final between Liverpool and Juventus. English clubs are banned from Europe as a result.

1988. The Football League celebrates its centenary with a Wembley festival of football.

1989. Hillsborough disaster.

Other leading players of the 1980s:

BRYAN ROBSON Manchester United and England's 'Captain Marvel' who won 90 caps for England and was a three-time FA Cup winning captain.

GARY LINEKER. England's goalscoring hero in the 1986 World Cup in Mexico. Lineker went on to score 48 goals for his country and, in one explosive season, notched 40 goals for Everton.

i belong to glasg

Says Celtic's HENRIK LARSSON

hENRIK LARSSON has assumed the rare mantle of torturer-in-chief of defences both north and south of the border.

At domestic level, Celtic striker Larsson is Scotland's Player of the Year, having terrorised Premier League defences with his displays of skill, speed and goalscoring.

While at international level, Larsson is Sweden's main man. He played a vital part in England's 2-1 Euro 2000 defeat in Stockholm.

Indeed, it was for a tackle on Larsson that Paul Ince was sent off in that first Group Five qualifier.

Playing regularly to Britain's biggest home crowd of 60,000 at Celtic Park, Henrik is the dreadlocked darling of the Hoops' support.

And, as he's more than happy to point out, he's content with life in Glasgow. So much so that he signed a new four-year contract with Celtic in the spring of 1999.

"Playing in front of so many fans every week is a brilliant feeling," grins Larsson.

"The fans are loud and when they shout and sing my name it makes me feel very proud. I know I must be doing well as fans don't sing for you unless you earn it.

"When I played in Holland, the Feyenoord fans used to sing my name, too, but there were never as many of them at matches.

"Since I arrived in Scotland the Celtic supporters have been fantastic to me.

"I'm settled and never thought I would leave Celtic. Why should I quit Scotland when I'm perfectly happy here?

"Being in Scotland is also good for my golf!"

Larsson finds it amusing that interest in his career extends to his performances for the Swedish national side.

Johan Mjallby - who netted the winner against England in Stockholm - is also a Hoops favourite and the two stars' international exploits have aroused much interest among Scots fans.

"It's good for both me and Celtic that I have a fellow Swede in Johan playing alongside me," reasons Larsson.

"He is a quality player who can play in a number of positions. He has played mainly as a defender for Celtic, but at international level he is used as an attacking midfielder - as England found out!

"He is a powerful presence and his goal in that game was very important.

"I can still remember my first day back at Celtic Park after that game.

"It was funny because everybody wanted to shake my hand and congratulate me on beating England. It just shows how big the rivalry is between the two countries.

"But I was just doing my job - I like to win every game I play in, no matter who it's against."

Last year, Larsson received the highest footballing accolade possible in his homeland - the mantle of Swedish Player of the Year.

He feels he won the award because he has matured as a player and because his time in Scotland has improved his all-round game.

"I feel as you get older you continually improve as a player," stresses the 27-year-old.

"My game has grown in lots of different ways since I arrived here, but I don't like to make comparisons between Scottish football and Holland where I played with Feyenoord.

"I think Scottish football is at a high level and there are opportunities to do even better in Europe.

"I don't feel the need to move again, having already gone from Sweden to Holland to Scotland.

"The move to Scotland actually helped my international career. When I first came here I wasn't in the international team.

"I am at an age where my game has matured and I feel Celtic, Sweden and I are benefiting.

"But I would hope there's still more to come. There's always room for improvement in everyone's game and I want to get even better."

What an ominous thought for defenders the length and breadth of Britain. ■

> "The move to Scotland actually helped my international career. When I first came here I wasn't in the international team."

OW!

DAVID UNSWORTH created a storm of controversy when he returned to Everton last season following a year's absence. The reason - he had signed for Aston Villa from West Ham earlier in the summer, and was leaving Villa Park without playing a single game for his new club.

Fans in the Midlands were quick to condemn him for turning his back on his new club so quickly. But Unsworth rode the storm, soon re-established himself on Merseyside, and was grateful when he at last received an encouraging response from some Villa fans who wished him luck.

As he looks back on the strange way in which he returned to his first club, he reflects that his year's absence did him good, yet he was pleased to find himself back on familiar territory.

Unsworth spent five years as a professional with Everton after signing for them as a teenager and was a first-team regular for most of that period.

"When I moved to West Ham, I wasn't very enthusiastic about leaving, but career-wise, I felt it was something which had to be done," he says.

"I wasn't on top of my form and had realised I was getting a bit stale. I'd been in the first team for four to five years and sometimes when a young player has such a run, it can have that effect.

"Going to Upton Park did me the world of good. I played first-team football week in and week out, was treated brilliantly by the fans and my overall confidence came back.

"The last thing I expected was that I would end up back where I started and pull on an Everton shirt again."

The manner of his return to Merseyside, however, was unusual to say the least. Reports at the time suggested the homesickness of his wife, Jane, was the motivating force which brought him north in stages, and the ridicule aimed at him for the quick change of mind which followed his transfer to Villa rankled for a while with the player.

"I made a professional mistake and I tried to rectify it by being honest to Everton, Aston Villa and the Villa fans," he recalls.

"It was a difficult decision to leave West Ham so soon after joining the club. I'd had twelve very happy months there and from the football point of view I felt very much at home among the other players and the fans.

"However, my family and I had found it very difficult to settle in the area and, away from the football club, we did not enjoy London life. We didn't know anybody down there and when my wife gave birth to our second daughter, we knew it would become more difficult.

"During the summer, we made a decision that the family would move back to the Merseyside area and, if the club were agreeable, I would commute from there to West Ham.

"However this didn't prove feasible. Then, other people became aware of the situation, and I heard through the grapevine that Everton were interested.

"However, it was Villa who made their bid first. West Ham were on a pre-season trip to Scotland and I was flown down to the Midlands to talk with them.

"Meanwhile, my agent was making Everton aware of the situation, and we expected them to follow up their interest.

"Unfortunately, manager Walter Smith and Chairman Peter Johnson were out of the country signing John Collins and Olivier Dacourt and communication with them broke down during the vital hours when the Aston Villa deal was being put together.

"We were expecting a call

> **"I realised that my desire to play for Everton was greater than anything else!"**

from Everton, but it never came.

"I had to make a decision and because I was getting no feedback from Goodison Park, I opted to sign for Villa.

"Hardly had the formalities been completed, however, than I learned that Everton's interest had not cooled at all. It turned out that, while we were negotiating with Villa, Walter Smith and Peter Johnson had been trying to get through to us, but couldn't because our phones were switched off."

When the truth dawned, it also sparked the change of heart and subsequent switch to Everton, which caused such consternation.

"When, having signed for Villa, Everton's interest was still apparent, I realised that my desire to play for them was greater than anything else, especially after the arrival of Walter as manager and Archie Knox as his assistant," adds David.

"So I decided that, professionally, the best thing for me to do was admit my mistake and try to smooth the path for a switch to Everton.

"Villa boss John Gregory was brilliant and sorted it all out for me. Without his help and guidance, it would not have been possible. Despite my change of heart, there was no animosity whatsoever.

"Some people tried to make out that the situation turned into a feud between us, but nothing could be further from the truth. It all ended amicably, and my transfer from Villa to Everton was completed.

"It was said that the main influence was my family's desire to live in Merseyside. But if I'd stayed with Villa, I would have been able to stay in this area and commute to Birmingham. So, it wasn't a family issue - it was me, as a professional, jumping at the chance of rejoining Everton." ■

107

RAY PARLOUR (Arsenal)

● BENITO CARBONE
(Sheffield Wednesday)

● DWIGHT YORKE
(Manchester United)

bite the du

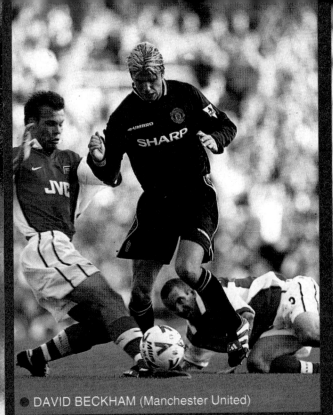
DAVID BECKHAM (Manchester United)

STEVE FROGGATT (Coventry City)

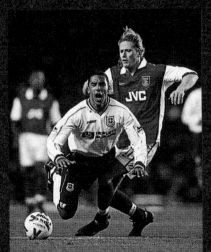
CHRIS ARMSTRONG (Spurs)

st!

Rushden and

king of diamonds

lifelong fan of Blackburn Rovers, he bankrolled the club to Championship success in 1995 and is still pumping millions in as they strive to get out of the First Division this season.

Max Griggs, however, went one better than the Rovers owner. He didn't just buy a club, he created a whole new one.

Griggs didn't realise what he was getting himself into when Tony Jones, the chairman of United Counties League side Irthingborough Diamonds, asked the Dr Martens footwear magnate to take over the club in 1992. Jones could not have picked anyone better to fill his boots in more ways than one.

Today, following his £20 million investment, Rushden and Diamonds of The Football Conference have facilities that are the envy of most Second and Third Division clubs.

All that is missing is a place in the League, something Griggs is determined to achieve before the season is out.

Says the retired businessman, "I wasn't that interested when Mr Jones originally spoke to me because I'd watched League football all my life and couldn't see myself enjoying football at such a low level.

YOU have just matched the six lottery numbers on a triple rollover week and you're a multi-millionaire. What are you going to spend your loot on? Faced with that dilemma, most football fans would be sorely tempted to buy into the football club they've always supported. It has to be the next best thing to actually playing.

That is precisely what Jack Walker did after selling his steel business a few years back. A

"Rushden and Diamonds. To me, that seemed to be a rather

"Trying to be helpful, though, I mentioned to Mr Jones that I might become involved if he talked with his counterpart at nearby Rushden Town with a view to merging the two clubs. To my amazement, they agreed and, all of a sudden, I was caught up in the enthusiasm and decided to give it a go.

"So I bought the ground from rthingborough Diamonds Supporters Club and amalgamated the two clubs under the name Rushden and Diamonds. To me, that seemed to be a rather long name but it was the only way to keep everyone happy.

"We started off the 1992/93 season in the Beazer Homes Midland Division with gates of 250. Within a couple of seasons, we won promotion to the Beazer Homes Premier League and the gates rose to 600. Two years later, we were in the Conference.

"Throughout that time, I was doing little bits and pieces to the place. When I arrived here, there was just an open field with a small clubhouse and railings all around the pitch.

"So I started to add a stand here and there, trying to build up a nice football ground for the future.

"I'm not the kind of person who plays at things. I wanted to do it properly. I made sure all the materials we used were of the highest quality. Nothing was done on the cheap.

"People said I was wasting my time. They reckoned it would just be vandalised.

"That hasn't been the case at all. In fact, there hasn't been one bit of graffiti on the walls or even a cigarette stub left on the ground. I believe that people respond well if they are treated properly.

"Once we were in the Conference, I put in another couple of stands until we have what is here now, a complete stadium.

"It is not just a football arena. We have banqueting halls, conference rooms, restaurants and a shop. It is more than just a football club.

"We're on 70 acres of land and I have plans for a cinema, a nightclub, a health and fitness centre and a hotel. I'm trying to umbrella the whole thing under the name Diamond City.

"I'm a local man and it is important to me that I have built something that the whole community can enjoy. My business has done well here and we employ a lot of local people so it is my way of putting a bit back in.

"You could say that if I hadn't became involved in this I'd have more money but, then, what would I do with it?

"I could have bought into a Premiership club if I'd wanted to but where is the fun in that? Premier League Chairman seem to have the troubles of the world

on their shoulders. I've had more fun building something from nothing at Rushden.

"Of course my wife thinks I'm mad. She reckons it takes up too much of my time. Sometimes she's right, especially when the team isn't doing so well.

"That is the thing with football. You can have the best intentions in the world but it doesn't always go to plan. Players might not perform as well as you'd hope or there might be a horrible run of injuries.

"I'm happy, though, so long as we can look back at the end of every season and see some progress. I think we've been able to do that so far.

"For instance, although we didn't win promotion this year, we did enjoy a fantastic FA Cup run, only losing out after a replay against mighty Leeds United. It was a brilliant time and earned the club and the business priceless exposure.

"This time winning the Conference and gaining promotion is THE aim. I always said that I wanted to get Rushden into the Football League by the year 2000 and I just hope I won't be left with egg on my face.

"Longer term, I want to build the club up slowly into a First Division outfit. That is a highly competitive level of football without the real hassles of the Premiership. I'd be happy with that." ■

ng name but it was the only way to keep everyone happy.❞

michael GRAY Sunderland

TOPICAL TIMES FOOTBALL BOOK

who am i?

Can you identify these five famous footballers?

1

2

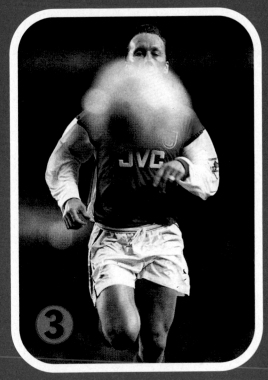

3

4

5

the long and

DANNY SONNER has made it at last!

DANNY SONNER always believed he could make it to the top as a footballer, but the Sheffield Wednesday midfielder certainly went around the houses before achieving his ambition.

Sonner is not your typical Premiership footballer. These days, most top professionals are nurtured at a big club from an early age with every intricate detail of their career planned out.

The likes of David Beckham and Michael Owen are fast-tracked to stardom, but Sonner's route to the top has been a long, winding road with various stopping-off points.

As a gifted youngster, Wigan-born Sonner expected the world to come to him. He knew he had the talent, but few football clubs were willing to test their patience to try to get the best out of Danny. Home-town club Wigan Athletic took a chance, but Sonner failed to break through. That rejection led to Danny trawling through the lower leagues with Burnley before a move to Germany kick-started his career.

He says, "It's a fair question to ask why I ended up at Burnley, but I have to be honest and say that I wasn't the easiest kid to deal with.

"I suppose I was a bit headstrong in my younger days. I wouldn't say that I was arrogant, but there were times when I said no to people when perhaps it would have been better to say yes.

"That's just the way I am, though. I could play football, but I was a bit hard to handle. As you get older, you realise where you went wrong, but I've done all right for myself so far.

"I didn't listen enough when I was a kid. I thought I was the bee's knees and that's why I didn't progress as I should have done.

"I did some daft things, like missing out on the chance to play for Manchester City. They invited me down to Maine Road for a trial, but I turned up on the wrong day!

"I eventually ended up at Burnley and for a while, I did well at Turf Moor. I enjoyed playing for the manager, Frank Casper, but when he was sacked things went downhill for me.

"His successor, Jimmy Mullen, was somebody I just did not get on with. I didn't like him, so when I was offered the chance to leave and go to Germany, I jumped at it.

"I was only 20 at the time, but I fancied a change and I went for it. Germany appealed to me. I was a young lad, but I was being offered very good money, an apartment and a car.

"It was a whole new experience for me and I really enjoyed it. The club I joined, Preussen Cologne, were in the Second Division and were managed by the former Nottingham Forest and England striker, Tony Woodcock.

"I had a good relationship with Tony and he sorted me out in many ways. He made me realise that I had to become more focussed if I was to achieve my ambitions.

"Some of my managers have found me difficult to get on with, but Tony understood me better than any boss I have worked for.

"I'm just a typical lad from a Wigan council estate, but Tony knew I was ambitious and he channelled me in the right direction. His influence was just what I needed at the time.

"I had three good years in Germany, the highlight being a cup win against Kaiserslautern. After scrapping and fighting in the English Third Division, it was good to play in a more technical environment.

"The experience broadened my mind, but when I was offered the chance of returning to England with Ipswich, I felt the time was right to come home."

> **If I had sunk without trace at Wednesday, nobody would have batted an eyelid.**

As part of the exciting young team at Portman Road, Sonner missed out on promotion to the Premiership by a hair's breadth on successive occasions.

His potential was spotted by Sheffield Wednesday manager Danny Wilson and Sonner moved to Hillsborough in October 1998 - for £75,000!

Many people were asking 'Danny Who?' but Sonner did not mind the fact that he cost less than some of the cars driven by his new team-mates.

All Danny was bothered about was taking the chance that he feared had passed him by.

He goes on, "When I joined Ipswich from Cologne, I was a free transfer under the Bosman ruling. Because I cost Ipswich nothing, I had a clause inserted in my contract which would allow me to move on for just £75,000.

"That paid off when Sheffield Wednesday wanted me because

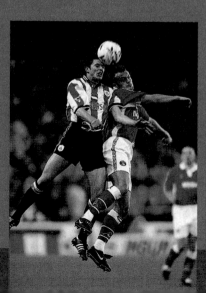

windingroad

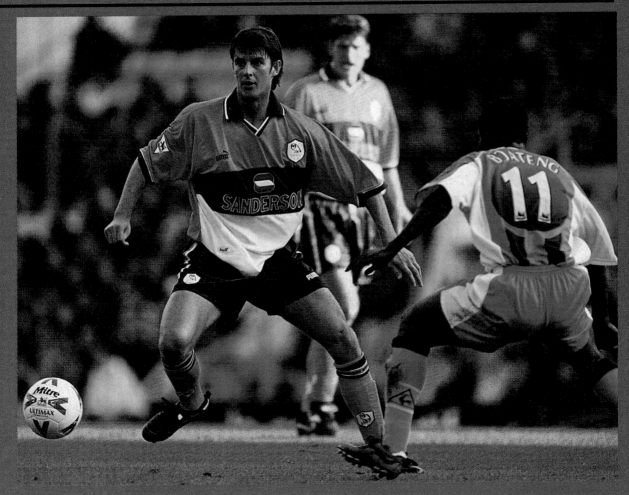

they were more than happy to spend such a small amount of money for me.

"It was fantastic for me as well because nothing was expected of me. Apart from the manager and my team-mates, nobody noticed me arriving at Hillsborough, so I had nothing to lose.

"If I had sunk without trace at Wednesday, nobody would have batted an eyelid. Having done quite well, though, people see me as a bargain.

"Hopefully, I have shown that you don't have to spend big money to find the right player. I am a £75,000 player playing in the Premiership, so it can be done.

Transfer fees are totally out of proportion these days and people have become obsessed with them.

"Coming to Sheffield has been great for me. Danny Wilson says that I am more suited to the Premiership than the lower leagues and I think he is right. The step up hasn't worried me at all.

"I always believed I was good enough to play at the top level among the best players, but I was beginning to wonder whether I would be overlooked because of my character and things that had happened in the past. I was always hopeful, but football can be a funny business and many good players don't get as high up the ladder as

they should.

"It isn't always the best players who make it. It's amazing how much luck plays a part. My lucky break was getting this move to Hillsborough.

"If I hadn't gone to Germany as a youngster, perhaps this move might never have happened. While over there, I realised that I had maybe only 10-15 years in the game and I asked myself whether I wanted it or not.

"I knew that I had to stay positive. If I had allowed myself to drop down the leagues I would never have reached the Premiership. I set my sights high and had a bit of luck on the way." ■

hamilton RICARD Middlesbrough

we're going up!

119

boss-man ruling!

Just call me Mr. President! says Celtic's VIDAR RISETH

t HERE ARE many things a footballer can do to secure his long-term future. Some earn coaching diplomas, others step into the media, while the more ambitious plough their considerable riches into business ventures. The possibilities for continuing their lavish lifestyles are endless.

However, Celtic star Vidar Riseth has set his sights even higher. The 27-year-old Norwegian internationalist has taken the unusual step of actually buying his own CLUB!

Riseth snapped up a majority stake in Norwegian Sixth Division side Vinger FC, after they approached him and asked for his help in getting them off the ground.

The enthusiastic Riseth, though, took things even further. Not only has he invested his own cash in the club, he also holds the position of club president, he is the part-time coach, and is currently seeking major sponsorship for the tiny Kongsvinger-based outfit.

"My involvement began when a friend of mine back home phoned me and asked if I wanted to start a club, saying he wanted me to be president," says Vidar.

"I said 'yes' and now we have signed 22 players between the ages of 27 and mid-30s who maybe cannot play at the top level any more but are all good, experienced players.

"I am the first Norwegian player to be a club president. That involves many things such as attracting sponsors but, because I am in the national team, companies call ME, asking how they can back the team.

"I became involved because I once played for Kongsvinger, a team in the town where Vinger are based.

"I am the first Norwegian player to be a club president."

"I have already bought a house there so that when I stop playing I can go there with my girlfriend, who is from the town."

Liverpool's Stig Inge Bjornebye is also from Kongsvinger and played 62 times for the club, scoring three times. Vidar hasn't got him involved - yet!

Despite his exciting venture into the business side of the game, Riseth insists that success with Celtic is still his number one priority.

"I have three years to go on my contract and I'm very happy. In fact, I would like to stay with Celtic even longer," he enthuses.

"But eventually I do plan to go back to Norway and play for Vinger FC when I feel I cannot play at the top level any more - maybe when I'm in my 30s."

Vidar goes on to reveal that the future is already looking bright for Vinger - on the field of play, as well as off it!

"We have the players training three nights a week, and we have beaten Third Division sides already. I'm sure we will go straight up to that division with the players we have and then we will not want to stop.

"Maybe by the time I go back to play we will get the club into the Premier Division." ∎

a century of soccer

no.7 1990-99

Player of the decade: Peter Schmeichel

HEN he was transferred to Manchester United from Brondby for a modest £550,000 back in 1991, few fans in England had heard the name Peter Schmeichel.

But it was not long before the Great Dane became accepted by many to be the best goalkeeper in the world, and his presence between their posts was a massive reason for United's dominance of the English football scene in the 1990s.

He has not always been popular, as controversy has followed him around. He once received death threats from Turkish extremists after he chased and caught a Galatasaray fan who ran across the Old Trafford pitch waving a blazing flag during a European Cup match in October, 1993.

He also attracted the nickname 'Mr Angry' due to his reputation for constantly shouting at his defenders and blaming anyone but himself for any goal conceded.

His ability remains unquestioned, however. No goalkeeper is more dominant in his penalty area and his very size has can intimidate opponents bearing down on goal.

Added to that, his agility and reflexes have enabled him to produce almost impossible saves.

His most celebrated was probably an incredible stop against Rapid Vienna in 1996 in the Champions League which was immediately compared with Gordon Banks' celebrated save from Pele in the 1970 World Cup.

Schmeichel even managed to score a last-minute equaliser against Rotor Volgograd in the UEFA Cup in 1995 to preserve the unbeaten home record in European competition which United cherished at the time.

He helped Denmark to win the 1992 European Championships and with United he won five Premiership titles, three FA Cups and a League Cup. His crowning moment, having just played his last domestic game for the club before retiring from English football last May, was to lift the European Cup as stand-in skipper on that memorable night in Barcelona.

Other leading players of the 1990s:

ERIC CANTONA. Enigmatic Frenchman who inspired Leeds United to the Championship in 1992, before moving across the Pennines to become the catalyst which ended Manchester United's long Championship drought. He won four Titles with them, plus two FA Cups.

ALAN SHEARER. England skipper who cost Newcastle United £15 million when they bought him from Blackburn Rovers. He had topped the 30 League goals in a season mark three years running with Rovers, winning the Title with them in 1995.

MARK HUGHES. Great battler for Manchester United, helping them to two Championships, three FA Cups and a European Cup Winners' Cup before moving to Chelsea where he added a record fourth FA Cup medal and another Cup Winners' Cup. Two League Cup winner's medals.

TONY ADAMS. Never-say-die Arsenal skipper, who has battled his way to three Championships, two FA Cups, two League Cups and a European Cup Winners' Cup.

Milestones:

1990 Peter Shilton retires as England goalkeeper with a world record 125 caps.
1992 Launch of the FA Premier League.
1995 Clubs are allowed to use three substitutes in one match. European Court of Justice upholds Bosman ruling, barring transfer fees for players out of contract.
1996 England lose to Germany in a semi-final penalty shoot-out in EURO 96.
1997 Ruud Gullit of Chelsea is the first foreign coach to win the FA Cup. Rangers emulate Celtic's record by winning nine Scottish Championships in a row.
1999 Manchester United complete an unprecedented treble of Premiership, FA Cup and European Cup.

ryan **GIGGS** Manchester United

TOPICAL TIMES FOOTBALL BOOK

picture list

ISBN 0 85116 702 0
Printed and Published in Great Britain by D. C. Thomson & Co. Ltd., 185 Fleet Street, London EC4A 2HS. © D. C. Thomson & Co. Ltd., 1999.

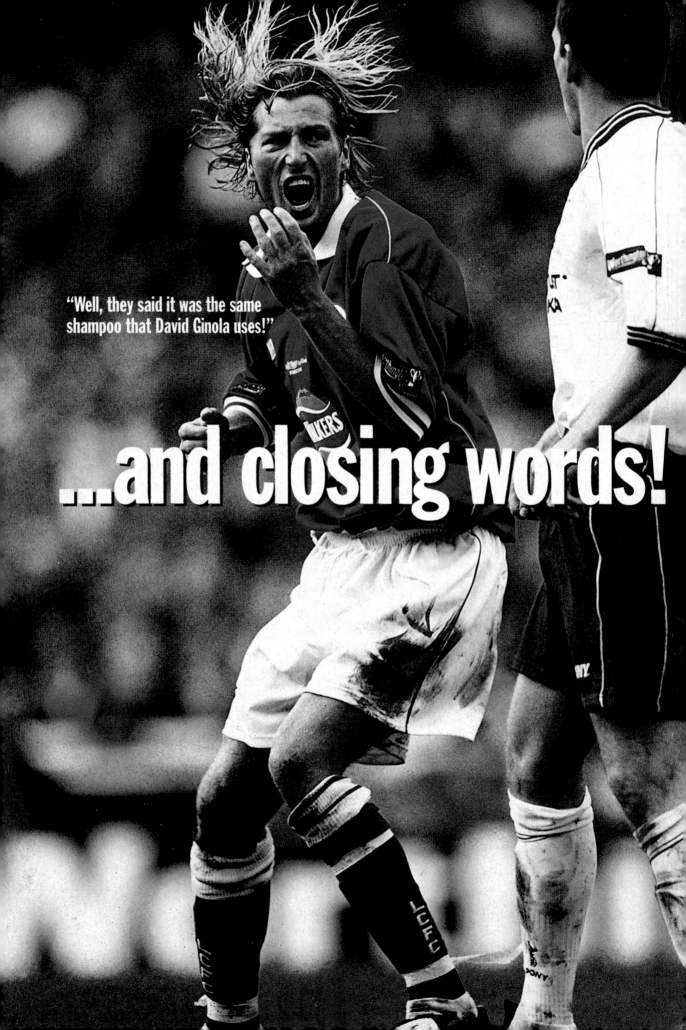

"Well, they said it was the same shampoo that David Ginola uses!"

...and closing words!